In the Country

250 years of country life in paintings, prose and poetry

Eileen Buckle and Derek Lord

NEW ENGLISH LIBRARY
TIMES MIRROR

Managing Editor: Pat Hornsey
Copy Editor: William J. Howell
Art Editor: Deborah Miles
Design: Mark Holt
Picture Research: Eileen Buckle and Derek Lord

This edition published in 1979 by New English Library Limited, Barnard's Inn, Holborn, London EC1N 2JR

© Text and illustrations copyright New English Library Limited 1979

Text set in Imprint by South Bucks Typesetters Limited
Headings to features in Garamond Bold Italic, photoset by Alphabet Limited
Printed by Fratelli Spada, Ciampino, Rome, Italy

450 04132 8

ACKNOWLEDGEMENTS

For permission to reprint the following items we are indebted to:

The Countryman[1] for 'Birds in a Changing Village'. *The Country-Side*[2] for 'Natural History by Train' and 'Motor Notes'. The estate of the late H. E. Bates and Laurence Pollinger Ltd for the extract from *In the Heart of the Country*. Austin Hatton and the *Sunday Telegraph* for 'Happy Families'. The estate of the late Henry Williamson and A. M. Heath & Co Ltd for 'Meadow Grasses'. J. H. B. Peel for 'Cavalcade of Summer Riches' – which is to be published in *Country Talk Continued* by Hale in December 1979. The estate of the late Mrs Frieda Lawrence Ravagli and Laurence Pollinger Ltd for 'The Rainbow'. Peter Jones and the Carcenet Press for 'Buttercups' and 'The Heron'. Ronald Blythe, Penguin Books and David Higham Associates Ltd for 'The Forge' from *Akenfield*. Anthony C. West for 'The Song of the Barrow', which appeared in *River's End*, Four Square Books. A. D. Peters & Co Ltd for the extract from Richard Keverne's *Tales of Old Inns*. The estate of the late Edmund Blunden and A. D. Peters & Co Ltd for the verses on hop-picking. The family of the late Denis Curling for 'The Cyclist' and 'Winter'.

We wish to thank Brian Coe of the Kodak Museum for the photographs of cyclists on page 69 and a wheelwright on page 176, and Surrey County Library for the photograph of Farnham Fair on page 59.

1 Subscription address: Watling Street, Bletchley, Milton Keynes, MK2 2BW
2 Subscription address: 40 Roundhill, Stone, Nr. Aylesbury, Bucks, HP17 8RD

Contents

'The Girl at the Gate' (1889) by Sir George Clausen (1852-1944); oils. (*Tate Gallery, London*)

Foreword

This is a book for country-lovers. It is for the country-dweller – and for town-dwellers who, like us, cannot get out into the country often enough. It is a book that is meant primarily to give enjoyment, and, as a substitute for the real thing, relaxation when you would like to escape to quiet places but cannot. In that role, you can explore with it all corners of the British Isles with well-known writers such as Dorothy Wordsworth in Scotland, George Borrow in Wales and T. H. Hudson in the West Country; or relive the delights of scaling Sna Fell with a mid-Victorian hiker who wrote about his experiences in a now defunct magazine.

The pictures, poems and prose have been selected from the rich cultural period that began about 250 years ago – a period which, with the Enclosure Act of the eighteenth century, gave rise to the country, criss-crossed by hedgerows, as we think of it today. We hope to take you back to the days when life was lived at a gentler pace, before mechanisation destroyed so much that was beautiful and wholesome. If we have tended to emphasise the happier side of life in the country it is not because we are unaware of the harsh realities of rural life, and especially of the poverty that was so widespread; nor have we ignored accompanying sadness. We are aware, too, that many of the changes that have taken place in the country are for the better, and hope that some of the items in this book will make that evident.

Regretfully, we have had to omit many items that we would have liked to include, for it is impossible in a book of this size to include *every* aspect of the country. We have attempted to build up a large picture out of a series of small pictures; inevitably, there are gaps. But, just as in a well-executed drawing the right impression comes across although not all the lines are included, we hope that imagination will fill the spaces.

'In Early Spring' (1854-5), detail, by John William Inchbold (1830-88); oils.
(*Ashmolean Museum, Oxford*)

Country Life Compared with Town Life

This article appeared in the issue dated 8 August 1868 of a magazine called *Country Life*, which was first published in 1865 (the present *Country Life* did not appear until 1897). Life in the towns compared unfavourably with that in the country the writer suggested, over a century ago. The 'wheel-clattering of Belgravia or Mayfair' of those days may have been irksome, but compared to the traffic noise of central London today it must have been relatively soothing to the ears

I HAVE found in conversation with some refined and cultivated townsmen that there was a general impression that Country Life tended to coarseness and vulgarity. That it was impossible to preserve that delicacy of manner and polite ease which are so much valued at the West End a dozen miles beyond the charmed Belgravian circle, unless, indeed, they visited some of the special districts consecrated to Fashion. Then, in the midst of a smaller though exactly similar circle to that they had left, they carried with them town manners, dresses, and habits; dined at the same hours, visited, shopped, told the same scandal, and played the same pieces on the piano, with croquet, flirtation, and so forth, exactly as in town the week previously. If by chance they encountered a plain, honest family – say that of a wealthy farmer, perhaps – they were shocked at the absence of conventional refinement, and set down their simple and unaffected manners to ignorance or vulgarity, forgetting that there is a vulgarity much worse than mere plainness of speech or awkwardness of motion – the vulgarity of mere finery.

The British Library, London

7

It would do some of our fashionable ladies much good if they would go occasionally into such neighbourhoods as Bethnal Green or Spitalfields. There are also some favourable localities in the direction of Poplar and the Isle of Dogs which may be recommended to their notice, and some remarkable specimens of the mother tongue catch the ear about Bermondsey and Leather Lane, which would astonish them not a little.

But our aristocratic friends will not judge the matter fairly. They see a few dirty tramps lounging at the door of a village inn, or sprawling under a hedge by the dusty wayside. They see a fat, red-faced labourer under the influence of a 'sunstroke', as it is humorously called this hot weather, but which could be better explained at the Coach and Horses, or Old Red Lion, taking a greater breadth of the pathway through the meadow than rightfully comes to his share, or filling up the towing path by the river in a perplexing way, which makes one hope that the water is not deep, or that our friend in his cups can swim. Or we may be disturbed sometimes just when we wished to hear the nightingale by that too noisy chorus from the Sons of Harmony at the Cross Roads beershop. But all this is completely on the surface. We can measure its length and breadth quite easily, the drawback is that it is so readily observed by the stranger.

But does one man or woman of ten thousand in high life know, understand, or believe the terrible life which is so near to them. There are few country cottages so filthy as to be absolutely repellant to a cultivated person, and there are few of their homely inhabitants who do not make some attempt at polishing up place and person if they receive any encouragement or sympathy from the class above them; but for real downright abandoned brutality – for life that shames the very beasts that perish – for life that seems heedless of a past and unconscious of a future – life defiant of law and order, kept only within the line of humanity by sternly repressive measures, we must seek the slums and dens of London. In this vast city, rich with the spoils of centuries, sending its beacon lights of science and discovery to the uttermost parts of the earth – great in its freedom, sublime in its power, unrivalled in its extent – it is in this labyrinth we must look if we would also discover human nature the most fallen, human instincts the most depraved, human passions the most fiendish, of any spot upon the habitable globe.

It may be safely said that, human nature left to itself – neglected, ignorant, coarse, though it be – does not, as a rule, sink so low as this in the country. And this is a fact which our lawgivers should remember. The isolation of the country gives greater prominence to the individual villain; but that the association of criminals breeds crime there is only too positive evidence in the state of our streets. Notwithstanding the number of police patrolling our thoroughfares by day and night, notwithstanding the strict watch and ward we keep upon our individual homes, how constant and horrible are the crimes of large cities! Can there be a more telling satire upon our boasted civilisation than the fact that we dare not trust our wives or sisters in even the most frequented streets without protection? Yet wilfully ignorant of all this, the Sybarite with his glass in his eye, and his scented handkerchief to his nostrils, shudders at a heap of manure by

From *The Graphic*, 8 June 1872

the wayside as he passes it in his carriage, and when he gets back to his beloved square or terrace tells, in lisping tones and with bated breath, the horrors of the country.

To such as these we leave the glories of the town, the fashionable promenade, the millhorse round of pleasure, 'and that unrest which men miscall delight'. Our sympathies are rather with those who seek the most secret and exquisite haunts of Nature, and who love them; who dwell with a dear delight upon the flood of sunshine sweeping over a golden field of corn, or a meadow blazing with buttercups in the early spring; who love the mysterious shadow of the forest and the music of the wind in the branches; who love the sudden shower pattering down between the roll of the distant thunder; who watch with subdued, but heartfelt pleasure, the sacred stillness of the falling snow; who, if they traverse wilder climes, are fully alive to the wonders of the pine-clad precipice, the creeping glacier, the fierce torrent; who discern amid the beauty something deeper and of wider import than the mere scenic effect of the theatre upon a vaster scale; who believe that in every age and clime, from the savage to the sage, God has left some sermon in the stone – some book in the running brook, full of meaning to those who will listen to their voices.

It appears to me most conclusive that the proportion of crime and worldliness must be greater where large masses of people are congregated together. Losing the wholesome and soothing effect which communion with nature has upon the senses, we are thrown backward upon personal influences. We are filled with those petty jealousies, passions, and caprices which grow so freely when humanity is cooped up in a narrow compass. Not only are we less tolerant of those who surround us when living a feverish and anxious life, but we suffer grievously in ourselves for want of that balance of the mind, that repose and firmness which a little thoughtfulness and contemplation will give.

A closer alliance with Nature would reduce the number of our fancied wants. Memory, instead of being, as it often is, a weariness, would become one of life's choicest gifts. It is because we have not enough pleasant memories that we so eagerly peer forward into the future, so eagerly clutch the present. Our remembrances are of something artificial, something not spontaneous or soothing. We have not after a life in the street a sense of growth about us; a sense of constant change and variety, coming and going without our aid, almost without our knowledge sometimes; a glory and a mystery equally beyond our rivalry or control. These magnificent images, these delightful impressions, these sacred associations, are not of the town, but God has bestowed them for the joy and wellbeing of those who can understand them. What is the great poet but the mouthpiece of Memory and Experience, and

The British Library, London

though it may be but the fortune of one in a million to make his keenness of observation universal, it is within the power of most to share to some extent his pleasurable feelings.

Especially with the great events of life we notice the dulling and hardening effect of the Town. The hearse and the railway van jostle each other in the march of modern civilisation; the ledger goes hand in hand with the Bible, and the sweet voices of childhood echo with the frantic curse of the sot and the despairing wail of the suicide. Humanity has no extremes that do not meet in the hurry and rush of this Babylonian strife. Children especially suffer from the loss of those associations in nature which stamp themselves ineffaceably upon the heart and affections, and make life seem sweeter and purer ever afterwards.

If, as many suppose, large towns swallowing up smaller centres, and ultimately sweeping away village life altogether, be the ultimate change for England, there is all the greater reason for some counteracting influence. We must go oftener than ever to Nature – not for amusement merely, but for her teaching – for that constant reference to first principles, without which there is

little real happiness. It is only thus we can feel our mortality less, our immortality more.

Nor is it necessary that we should possess the creative gifts of a great poet to comprehend the sweet underlying lessons of Nature. Thousands of meaner capacity drink in the inner spirit of Nature, though unable to give any active sign of the influence which makes their lives and everyday actions purer and more elevated. To such as these life has mysteries, depths, revelations, which come not in the illuminated brilliancy of the ballroom; they hear a music never echoed at the Opera – are conscious of a movement which has nothing in common with the wheel-clattering of Belgravia or Mayfair. To them birth and death is something more than the unit more or less in the census, and while society, looking through its worldly microscope, sees greatly magnified the trumpery little things at its feet, they calmly gaze with naked eyes at the loftier heights attainable to humanity.

While writing this sketch I chanced to meet with a clever little book, by an American author, entitled *Walden; or, Life in the Woods*. It is by an eminent author who, becoming weary of the mechanical life of the large towns, adopted an entirely rustic life. In the following extract he says:

I went to the woods because I wished to live deliberately, to front only the essential facts of life, and see if I could not learn what it had to teach, and not, when I come to die, discover that I had not lived. I did not wish to live what was not life, living is so dear; nor did I wish to practise resignation unless it was quite necessary. I wanted

Some children from London slums enjoy a day in the country. From *The Graphic*, 29 June 1872.

to live deep and suck out all the  marrow of life, to live so sturdily and Spartan-like as to put to rout all that was not life, to cut a broad swath and shave close, to live life into a corner, and reduce it to its lowest terms, and, if it proved to be mean, why then to get the whole and genuine measure of it, and publish its meanness to the world; or if it were sublime, to know it by experience, and be able to give a true account of it in my next excursion. For most men, it appears to me, are in strange uncertainty about it.

I did not read books the first summer; I hoed beans. Nay, I often did better than this. There were times when I could not afford to sacrifice the bloom of the present moment to any work, whether of the head or hands. I love a broad margin to my life. Sometimes, on a summer morning, having taken my accustomed bath, I sat in my sunny doorway from sunrise to noon, wrapt in a reverie, admidst the pines, and hickories, and sumachs, in undisturbed solitude and stillness, while the birds sang around or flitted noiseless through the house, until, by the sun falling in at my west window, or the noise of some traveller's wagon on the distant highway, I was reminded of the lapse of time. I grew in those seasons like corn in the night, and they were far better than any work of the hands would have been ... My days were not days of the week, bearing the stamp of any heathen deity, nor were they minced into hours and fretted by the ticking of a clock; for I lived like

the Puri Indians, of whom it is said that, 'for yesterday, today, and tomorrow, they have only one word, and they express the variety of meaning by pointing backward for yesterday, forward for tomorrow, and overhead for the passing day.' This was sheer idleness to my fellow-townsmen, no doubt; but if the birds and flowers had tried me by their standard, I should not have been found wanting. A man must find his occasions in himself, it is true. The natural day is very calm, and will hardly reprove his indolence.

Human nature, however noble, is full of strange caprices, and is rarely satisfied with the attainment of its most earnest desires. We look over the low hill which seemed so easy to climb, only to find a higher and still a higher beyond. When this endless craving reveals to us that there is something deeper and more true for which we were created, and toward which our daily march is tending; when we find that the pursuit of wealth or fame, even if succcssful, leaves us as unsatisfied as ever; when we feel with shame and remorse that we have too often neglected some nobler duty that would have hindered our selfish progress for the moment; when we feel distanced in some narrow rivalry or defeated in some favourite scheme, there is always the great Mother ready to lead us back to her sweet inheritance of simple pleasures and quiet minds; always ready in language older than the language of man to speak peace to the weary heart and the jaded brain.

Violeting

BY MARY RUSSELL MITFORD (1787-1855)

Mary Russell Mitford provided an animated description of English rural life during the closing years of the Georgian era. Her book *Our Village*, from which this is an excerpt, was based on Three Mile Cross, near Reading

MARCH 27th – It is a dull grey morning, with a dewy feeling in the air; fresh, but not windy; cool, but not cold: the very day for a person newly arrived from the heat, the glare, the noise, and the fever of London, to plunge into the remotest labyrinths of the country, and regain the repose of mind, the calmness of heart, which has been lost in that great Babel. I must go violeting . . . a few yards farther, and I reach the bank.

Ah! I smell them already – their exquisite perfume steams and lingers in this moist, heavy air. Through this little gate, and along the green south bank of this green wheat-field, and they burst upon me, the lovely violets, in tenfold loveliness. The ground is covered with them, white and purple, enamelling the short dewy grass, looking but the more vividly coloured under the dull, leaden sky. There they lie by hundreds, by thousands. In former years I have been used to watch them from the tiny green bud, till one or two stole into bloom. They never came on me before in such a sudden and luxuriant glory of simple beauty – and I do really owe one pure and genuine pleasure to feverish London! How beautifully they are placed too, on this sloping bank, with the palm branches waving over them, full of early bees, and mixing their honeyed scent with the more delicate violet odour! How transparent and smooth and lusty are the branches, full of sap and life! And there, just by the old mossy root, is a superb tuft of primroses, with a yellow butterfly hovering over them, like a flower floating on the air. What happiness to sit on this tufty knoll, and fill my basket with the blossoms! What a renewal of heart and mind! To inhabit such a scene of peace and sweetness is again to be fearless, gay, and gentle as a child. Then it is that thought becomes poetry, and feeling religion. Then it is that we

13

are happy and good. Oh, that my whole life could pass so, floating on blissful and innocent sensation, enjoying in peace and gratitude the common blessings of Nature, thankful above all for the simple habits, the healthful temperament, which render them so dear! Alas! who may dare expect a life of such happiness? But I can at least snatch and prolong the fleeting pleasure, can fill my basket with pure flowers, and my heart with pure thoughts; can gladden my little home with their sweetness; can divide my treasures with one, a dear one, who cannot seek them; can see them when I shut my eyes; and dream of them when I fall asleep.

Sweet Violets: from the sketchbook of M. E. Morris, late 19th century.
(*By courtesy of the Victoria and Albert Museum, London. Photograph: Brian Hunt; John Freeman & Co*)

Our Village by a Villager

BY THOMAS HOOD (1799-1845)

Thomas Hood, born in London, was of Scottish descent. In the following poem, the charmingly erratic, conversational style of Mary Russel Mitford is delightfully parodied

Our village, that's to say not Miss Mitford's village,
    but our village of Bullock Smithy,
Is come into by an avenue of trees, three oak
    pollards, two elders, and a withy;
And in the middle, there's a green of about not
    exceeding an acre and a half;
It's common to all, and fed off by nineteen cows,
    six ponies, three horses, five asses, two foals,
    seven pigs, and a calf!
Besides a pond in the middle, as is held by a
    similar sort of common-law lease,
And contains twenty ducks, six drakes, three
    ganders, two dead dogs, four drown'd kittens,
    and twelve geese.
Of course the green's cropt very close, and does
    famous for bowling when the little village boys
    play at cricket;
Only some horse, or pig, or cow, or great jackass,
    is sure to come and stand right before the wicket.
There's fifty-five private houses, let alone barns
    and workshops, and pigstyes, and poultry huts,
    and suchlike sheds;
With plenty of public houses – two Foxes, one
    Green Man, three Bunch of Grapes, one Crown,
    and six King's Heads.
The Green Man is reckon'd the best, as the only

15

one that for love or money can raise
A postilion, a blue jacket, two deplorable lame
    white horses, and a ramshackled 'neat postchaise'.
There's one parish church for all the people,
    whatsoever may be their ranks in life or their
    degrees,
Except one very damp, small, dark, freezing-cold,
    little Methodist chapel of Ease;
And close by the churchyard there's a stonemason's
    yard, that when the time is seasonable
Will furnish with afflictions sore and marble urns
    and cherubims very low and reasonable.
There's a cage, comfortable enough; I've been in
    it with old Jack Jeffrey and Tom Pike;
For the Green Man next door will send you in ale,
    gin, or anything else you like.
I can't speak of the stocks, as nothing remains of
    them but the upright post;
But the pound is kept in repairs for the sake of
    Cob's horse, as is always there almost.
There's a smithy of course, where that queer sort
    of a chap in his way, Old Joe Bradley,
Perpetually hammers and stammers, for he
    stutters and shoes horses very badly.
There's a shop of all sorts, that sells everything,
    kept by the widow of Mr Task;
But when you go there it's ten to one she's out of
    everything you ask.
You'll know her house by the swarm of boys, like
    flies, about the old sugary cask:
There are six empty houses, and not so well
    paper'd inside as out.
For bill-stickers won't beware, but stick notices of
    sales and election placards all about.
That's the Doctor with a green door, where the
    garden pots in the windows is seen;
A weakly monthly rose that don't blow, and a
    dead geranium, and a tea-plant with five black
    leaves and one green.

As for hollyoaks at the cottage doors, and
    honeysuckles and jasmines, you may go and whistle;
But the Tailor's front garden grows two cabbages,
    a dock, a ha'porth of pennyroyal, two
    dandelions, and a thistle.
There are three small orchards — Mr Busby's the
    schoolmaster's is the chief —
With two pear-trees that don't bear; one plum and
    an apple, that every year is stripped by a thief.
There's another small day-school too, kept by the
    respectable Mrs Gaby.
A select establishment, for six little boys and one
    big, and four little girls and a baby;
There's a rectory, with pointed gables and strange
    odd chimneys that never smokes,
For the rector don't live on his living like other
    Christian sort of folks;
There's a barber's, once a week well-filled with
    rough black-bearded, shock-headed churls,
And a window with two feminine men's heads,
    and two masculine ladies in false curls;
There's a butcher's, and a carpenter's, and a
    plumber's, and a small green-grocer's, and a baker,
But he won't bake on a Sunday, and there's a
    sexton that's a coal-merchant besides, and an
    undertaker;
And a toy-shop, but not a whole one, for a village
    can't compare with the London shops;
One window sells drums, dolls, kites, carts, bats,
    Clout's balls, and the other sells malt and hops.
And Mrs Brown, in domestic economy not to be a
    bit behind her betters,
Lets her house to a milliner, a watchmaker, a
    rat-catcher, a cobbler, lives in it herself, and it's
    the post office for letters.
Now I've gone through all the village — ay, from
    end to end, save and except one more house,
But I haven't come to that — and I hope I never
    shall — and that's the Village Poor House!

Birds in a Changing Village

BY W. L. SMITH DRAWINGS BY KEITH BROCKIE

This contemporary description of bird life in the country originally appeared in the Summer 1978 edition of *The Countryman*. Founded in 1927, this magazine is published quarterly from Burford, in Oxfordshire

S A BOY twenty-five years ago I lived on the outskirts of a Berkshire village, itself on the edge of the well-wooded and curiously remote central part of the county. Although the house was only a few miles from a large town, it was very much a rural rather than a suburban environment and we always thought of ourselves as country dwellers and not townspeople. At that time I spent a lot of my spare time in watching birds and covered the immediate surroundings of my parents' home fairly intensively. Recently I have returned to the district rather more frequently than for some years, and this has prompted me to reflect on the changes in the bird life of this small area since I was a boy.

In this district there are two main types of habitat: one, an area of woodland, spinneys and thickets; and the other a system of large old fields, poorly drained, never ploughed, and used, if at all, only as rough grazing for cattle, and latterly horses. These fields are bounded on one side by a stream flowing into the Thames, and are known collectively as the marsh. They have never been really marshy in my lifetime, but twenty-five years ago they remained wet in parts all the year round, with a shallow ditch, excavated as a tank-trap during the last war, running across them. This whole area now seems to have become much drier, and the tank-trap and other drainage ditches appear to be spontaneously filling themselves in, as such channels tend to do unless regularly dredged out.

To me this countryside has deteriorated since I was a lad, but not as rapidly as I once feared, and the bird life, especially to one like myself who now lives in the suburbs of a large city, is still very rich. During a recent long weekend, in which bird-watching was very much a secondary preoccupation, we recorded nearly fifty different species without effort. Since the early 1950s the town has encroached on the country, but not

'Primroses and a Bird's Nest' by William Henry Hunt (1790-1864); watercolour.
(*Tate Gallery, London. Photograph: John Webb*)

Skeletons of dead elms . . . Keith Brockie. (*The Countryman*)

to a major extent; houses now cover one of the lowest fields nearest the village and part of the old allotments, but building elsewhere has not been conspicuous. The area has however suffered in other ways: barbed-wire fencing has spread widely, and hedgerows, if not removed, appear to be more severely pruned than they were. Hedgerow trees are tending to be removed, or (a surprising number over the years) blown down, and the gaunt skeletons of dead elms are only too common.

Overhead wires have also become prominent, and there is more noise than there used to be. The district is in a peculiarly unfavourable position in this respect, with the new M4 motorway not far to the south, the main Western Region railway line (now with high-speed trains) to the north, and overhead a stream of airline traffic, fortunately still quite high up, flying in to London Airport. As a result of all these changes it is not perhaps surprising that the touch of wilderness that used to linger on in some parts of this district has now gone.

Much of the woodland is, however, still intact, and in some parts changed for the better. The Forestry Commission took over a lot of it some time ago, cut down a fine wood of beech-trees, but also cleared out a couple of rather scruffy damp copses by the stream and replanted with poplars. All the forestry plantations have grown well, with an increasingly dense understorey of brambles, thorn and other thicket growth which seems to be becoming more favourable to bird life than the copses they have replaced.

One can summarise by saying that in the woodlands the bird life has held its own, and even flourished, but that of the open country has deteriorated both in variety and quantity. In the fields forming the marsh, snipe, partridge and lapwing used to be common, and in one exceptionally wet season redshanks appeared. The first three species now appear to have gone, at least as common residents, and the pleasant rasp of the partridge and the drumming of unseen snipe are no longer the familiar sounds of spring twilights. This decline has been accelerated, I suspect, not only by the drying-out of the fields, but also in the case of snipe and partridge by the spread of barbed wire, which must be particularly hazardous to birds with a habit of flying fast and low over the ground when disturbed.

The marsh used to be full of interest; I once disturbed a water rail perching, or stuck, about five feet up in a boundary hedgerow. At strategic points in and around it are low concrete blockhouses built during the last war as invasion defences. After the war a half-hearted attempt was made to demolish these pillboxes, but only one was effectively blown apart, and the masses of shattered concrete and tangled iron reinforcement still lie there. These ruins never became the focus of wild life that I half-expected (they exerted too great a fascination over the local boys), but I once found a stockdove's nest in a tree beside them. The stockdoves as well seem to have faded away, but their place has been taken by collared-doves, which were quite unknown in the district in the early 1950s.

The stream flowing beside the marsh is still quite clear and full of fish, and its bird life does not appear to have greatly altered. Wagtails, swallows, moorhens and the occasional little grebe are still present, mallard are as common as ever and the odd kingfisher is still to be seen.

The greatest population of birds is still found, as it used to be, in the area of woodland, large gardens and more open

Pheasant in a daffodil patch: Keith Brockie. (*The Countryman*)

country with isolated thickets and old hedgerows. Willow warblers are flourishing in the damp poplar woods established by the Forestry Commission, and nightingales have also moved in, in places where they were once only rarely heard. Red-backed shrikes, a couple of pairs of which could normally be found in the summers of the early 1950s, went some years ago, and white-throats more recently.

Most other species have at least held their own, and some have increased. Jays, for example, seem decidedly more common, as do goldfinches, bullfinches and wrens. Nuthatches and treecreepers are perhaps seen more often than they used to be, but green woodpeckers are much scarcer. Barn owls were always rare, and I have heard of no recent sighting; tawny and little owls are still present, but the latter species has lost ground. Pheasants are flourishing, perhaps as a result of artificial breeding, which may also be responsible for their increasingly confiding nature (last year a clutch of fifteen eggs was laid in a garden in a daffodil patch only a few yards from the window of a house).

One often reads about the increasing pressure on the countryside, but it seems to me that this pressure develops in a very erratic way. Well-advertised places and readily accessible viewpoints are certainly inundated with an increasing number of visitors, and there is of course no doubt that many more people, for example, climb Snowdon each weekend than was the case thirty years ago. Nevertheless, my own experience of this fragment of ordinary countryside is that fewer people go into some parts of it than they used to in my childhood. The bank of the stream was once crowded with family parties on a fine summer's day; now there are only a few. It was the custom of my family, like that of many others, to go for a walk in the country on Sunday afternoons, and such walks were a string of encounters with other people out for a similar purpose. The habit of Sunday walks now seems to have practically disappeared, and the number of groups of boys who roam the fields has similarly decreased.

In some of the more wooded parts particularly, there has been, as a result of these changing customs, a reversion to a state of less disturbance which has been beneficial to wild life. I was struck with this recently when I found a rather conspicuous greenfinch's nest with eggs in an isolated bush, very close to what used to be a busy footpath. This nest would not have lasted long in my youth; the village boys would soon have found it out.

Nature is resilient, and soon returns when man retreats. Birds seem to have the additional ability of adjusting to change by modifying their habits. Mag-

Reed buntings into arable farmland . . . Keith Brockie. (*The Countryman*)

pies have moved into suburban gardens from their traditional home in wooded countryside, and reed buntings into arable farmland from wet reedbeds. If bird life is given enough time to adapt in this way, and if farmers and others can be persuaded to leave patches of untended thicket growth on their land, there is some hope that the variety of birds in the Berkshire countryside and elsewhere will not deteriorate too much in the next twenty-five years.

Fruit Blossom Time

FROM *IN THE HEART OF THE COUNTRY* BY H. E. BATES (1905-74)

Novelist and short-story writer, H. E. Bates sympathetically evoked the countryside in some of his works. He also wrote about the war in Burma and about the RAF during the Second World War under the pseudonym 'Flying Officer X'

THE orchards begin to move into life as far back as February, sometimes in January, in warm winters in December: not cherries or plums or apples, but orchards of hazel, which hang out avenues of slanting, honey-green catkins that seem smokily luminous in the flat winter sun.

In the whole English fruit year there is nothing quite like this first soft wintry blossoming of millions of catkins, when countless flowers swing away from the wind together and stand out horizontally in air, poised in golden parallel, almost flying, then falling away and dancing in the moments of dead calm.

The avenues are so straight and formal and the pruning of the trees so rigid that the catkins seem like irresponsible things, too frisky and delicate for squat trees pruned of their grace. And I imagine hardly anyone ever sees these first nut orchards blooming in mid-winter; and I imagine, too, that for every hundred persons who see them only one, perhaps, sees their millions of other flowers: the almost invisible firmament of minute female flowers, like ragged scarlet stars, that hide behind the dancing curtains of the males.

Between these early orchards and the real bonfires of blossom there is a gap of a month or more. In the old orchards of the south it is partly filled – you might almost say illuminated – by snowdrops. They suddenly cover the old winter grass everywhere, white crops of petals, like flakes, drifting thickly sometimes among the sheep-pens, where first lambs hobble from behind the wind-breaks of yellow straw. And towards the end of March, or early in April, geese will replace the whiteness of both lambs and snowdrops. They seem to like orchards, and come back year after year to build their nest in the same place, guarded with fierce and rather comic devotion, under the budding trees.

I am writing of the south, where in many districts plums and cherries predominate over apples, and where few pears, except the delicious long green Conference, are grown, and it would be hard to say which blooms first, cherry or plum. I think perhaps the earliest plums break first, creamy-headed and never

23

'Cherry blossom comes in royally in heavy clustered sheaves', an illustration for *In the Heart of the Country* by C. F. Tunnicliffe. (*Country Life Limited*)

really white even when open, but always  cherries is said to compensate handsomely for two that are bad. And it is strange that with the fruit colouring so differently – pink, cream, scarlet, black – there is no corresponding variation of flower colour. Even the little black Morellas, flowering and fruiting rather late and less heavily than the ordinary kinds, have still that pure, constant whiteness.

touched a little with green and cream. The April distances still being sombre, the plum orchards are almost always a misty surprise when seen from afar off, half melting into the breaks of the land, entirely melting into a sky of broken cloud. They will be seen at their best from hilltops or against hillsides, and at their very richest when the Victorias bloom, with their larger blossoms of pure dazzling whiteness, against which all other plums seem like faded ivory.

It is the apples that break the rule of whiteness, by which pears are also governed, though the fat pear-blossom buds are sometimes almost golden, with the honey touch of pears themselves. But there are few pear orchards and, unhappily in England, no peach orchards. In the apple orchards alone is there a break into colour. Shades of pink deepen and pale all through the range of apple varieties: the silver-pink of shells; the cool pink of wild roses; the true, clear, wild, crab-pink; the deep vermilion-pink of some large late-flowered variety like Lord Derby.

But if the plum orchards have a certain laciness, so much part of the sketchy April scene of half-colours and quickly changing light, the cherry orchards have a rich and glorious solidity. They seem like a festival. Plum bloom is sprinkled along the bough, but cherry bloom comes in royally in heavy clustered sheaves, bountifully, and yet, because of the long flower-stalk, with grace and lightness; the trees are bigger, sometimes vast, the bloom bursts in great festoons from every bough, and the whole blossoming is like a harvest of flower. There is nothing – in England, at any rate – like the flowering of the cherry orchards in the first days of May, so prodigious and magnificent that the white branches are sometimes weighed down, as if by fruit, on the extreme orchard edge, where sun ripens the fruiting wood and in July brings the white-hearts swinging down to the dog-roses in the hedgeside.

And so the apples, coming last, are to my mind – in spite of Housman – the loveliest of trees. The blossoming of apples is warmer, more summery; it is an individual as well as a collective thing. The cherry has in it a touch of northern snowy beauty; its loveliness comes entirely from the white wonder of the great shining masses of flower. But each apple flower has individuality: a buttonhole flower, friendly; that you feel you must break off and cherish and smell. For there is no sweetness like the clear, affectionate fragrance of apple bloom, pure and delicate and joyous, blown in over the edge of summer.

No one who has ever seen that prodigious snowiness of the cherry orchards will doubt that cherry-land has sometimes ten times the value of the best farmland, and that one good season of

'In a Shoreham Garden' (c 1829) by Samuel Palmer (1805-81); watercolour plus body colour. (*By courtesy of the Victoria and Albert Museum, London. Photograph: Brian Hunt; John R. Freeman & Co*)

The Maypole

FROM *THE RETURN OF THE NATIVE* BY THOMAS HARDY (1840-1928)

Born and bred in Dorset, Hardy drew from his own experiences when capturing rural life in south-west England in his romantic novels

IT was a lovely May sunset, and the birch trees which grew on this margin of the vast Egdon wilderness had put on their new leaves, delicate as butterflies' wings, and diaphanous as amber. Beside Fairway's dwelling was an open space recessed from the road, and here were now collected all the young people from within a radius of a couple of miles. The pole lay with one end supported on a trestle, and women were engaged in wreathing it from the top downwards with wild flowers ... Yeobright did not interrupt the preparations, and went home again. The next morning, when Thomasin withdrew the curtains of her bedroom window, there stood the Maypole in the middle of the green, its top cutting into the sky. It had sprung up in the night, or rather early morning, like Jack's beanstalk. She opened the casement to get a better view of the garlands and posies that adorned it. The sweet perfume of the flowers had already spread into the surrounding air, which, being free from every taint, conducted to her lips a full measure of the fragrance received from the spire of blossom in its mist. At the top of the pole were crossed hoops decked with small flowers; beneath these came a milk-white zone of May bloom; then a zone of bluebells, then of cowslips, then of lilacs, then of ragged-robins, daffodils, and so on, till the lowest stage was reached. Thomasin noticed all these, and was delighted that the May-revel was to be so near.

May Day Revels by Myles Birket Foster (1825-99). (*The British Library, London*)

The Hawthorn

BY JAMES BRITTEN, FLS

The author, a Fellow of the Linnean Society, wrote several books and numerous articles on botanical subjects. In Chelsea, in London, where he was born, there is Britten Street, named after his father in recognition of his local activities

IN writing of a plant so universally familiar, there is no necessity to occupy either time or space by a botanical description. Such may be found in any book treating of British plants; and our present aim is rather to interest our general readers by some notes upon the popular history of the hawthorn, than to enter upon a description of the various forms, or varieties, which it presents to the botanist.

From very early times in our English history, the hawthorn, or May, as it is also frequently called, has played a prominent part in the festivities with which the month whose name it bears was ushered in. The custom of carrying round garlands upon May-day, which, in spite of the 'march of intellect', is still general in many parts of the country, is but a remnant of former days, when 'going a Maying' was the almost universal occupation of great and small; when, as Herrick tells us, each field became a street,

> Each street a park
> Made green and trimmed with trees! see how

> Devotion gives each house a bough
> Or branch! Each porch, each doore,
> ere this
> An arke, a tabernacle is,
> Made up of whitethorne neatly
> enterwove.

when the 30th of April was entered in the calendar as the day 'when the boys go out and seek May trees'; and when, on May-day, it was the custom of the Eton boys, the weather being fine, and leave being given, to rise at four o'clock and gather May branches, if they could do it without wetting their feet. But this was three hundred years ago; and one can scarcely imagine the modern Etonian availing himself of this permission, even if it were granted. Chaucer, in his 'Court of Love', speaking of May-day, says, 'Fourth goth al the Court, both most and lest, to fetche the flouris fresh, and braunch, and blome'; and it is on record that Henry VIII and Queen Catherine, with their courtiers, took part in this diversion.

The change in the calendar, however, and the consequent advance of May-day by twelve days, have rendered the whitethorn by no means a characteristic feature in the garlands prepared for the occasion. Indeed, it is seldom that any quantity of blossoms appears by that date, though Miller tells us that in 1783 it began to flower on the 21st of March, and Gilbert White, in his Selborne calendar, notes it for the 20th of April. It is usually, however, from the middle to the end of the month that we may best, with Chaucer,

Mark the fair beauty of the hawthorn tree,
Who, finely clothed in a robe of white,
Feeds full the wanton eye with May's delight.

The exceptional time of flowering of one variety of the hawthorn, and the legend connected with it, cannot be passed over in a paper like the present. We refer to what is known as the 'Glastonbury thorn', which tradition tells us sprang from the staff of St Joseph of Arimathea, who came to England and placed it in the ground, and, on waking, found it grown into a tree, covered with white blossoms – a story which, by the way, recalls to us one of the tales of the brothers Grimm, of which it may be a localised version. Be that as it may, it seems certain that the first Christian church in England was built upon the spot where the thorn is said to have stood; and that the tree to which the legend was attached, or a descendant of it, remained a wonder to many generations. It was reported to bud on Christmas eve, to be in full flower on Christmas morning, and withered the same night; and, without any belief in this rapid transition, we may fairly suppose that about Christmas-time the tree was in blossom. Such an occurrence is by no means isolated: we have seen in the park, at High Wycombe, a small hawthorn which every year produced buds in December and, in 1869, put forth fragrant fully-expanded blossoms at the end of that month. Our Glastonbury thorn, however, had a reputation extending beyond England – pieces of it were exported by the Bristol merchants to foreign lands, and much prized. Nor must it be supposed that this belief in the marvel was confined to what are termed the dark ages. Queen Anne, as well as many of the nobility of her time, bought slips of the tree at a high price; and pilgrimages were made to it as late as the beginning of the eighteenth century. One of the two trunks was cut down by a Puritan in the time of Elizabeth, and the other in the reign of Charles I, but a slip was secured, and inherited the peculiarity of the parent, which is shared by two old hawthorns, doubtless descendants, still standing within the precincts of Glastonbury Abbey. At the time of the introduction of the 'new style', the Glastonbury thorn attained great popular importance, from the fact that it remained firm to its old custom, and came into leaf or flower on 'Old Christmas Day'. We read in the *London Evening Post*, for January, 1753, that 'a vast concourse of people attended the noted thorn on Christmas Day, new style; but there was no appearance of its blowing, which made them all watch it narrowly, till the fifth of January, the Christmas Day, old style, when it blowed as usual'. It is said that people were sent from various parts of the country to consult the tree, and the support which it gave to the popular prejudice against the alteration of the calendar was very considerable.

On the same evening, at Quainton, in Buckinghamshire (says the *Gentleman's Magazine*), above two thousand people went, with lanterns and candles, to view a blackthorn (*sic*) in that neighbourhood, and which was remembered to be a slip from the famous Glastonbury thorn, and that it always budded on the 24th, was full blown the next day, and went all off at night.

No appearance of a bud was found, and we are told that the people consequently refused to recognise the new Christmas Day, and so firmly adhered to their determination that the ministers of the neighbouring villages, in order to appease them gave notice that the old Christmas Day should be kept holy as before.

Many traditions, indeed, cluster round the hawthorn. Miss Pratt tells us of one, still living, at Cawdor Castle, which is of great antiquity. Tradition relates that the original proprietor of the edifice was directed by a dream to build a castle exactly on the spot, and this was done in such a manner as to leave no doubt that the tree existed long before the structure was reared. The trunk of the tree with its knotted protuberances is in a vaulted apartment at the base of the principal tower, its root branching out beneath the floor, and its top penetrating the vaulted arch of the stone above in such a manner that any person seeing it would feel assured that the masonry was adjusted to the size and form of the tree, a space being left at the top of the vaults through which its boughs might be reared. From the most remote times it had been customary for guests to assemble themselves around this tree, and drink success to the house of Cawdor. A thorn, planted by Mary, Queen of Scots, in the garden of the Regent Murray's house is still, or was till recently, in existence. Another historical hawthorn is that which Goldsmith has immortalised in *The Deserted Village*:

> The hawthorn tree, with seats
>   beneath the shade,
> For talking age or whispering lovers
>   made.

This aged tree, which existed until about sixty years since in Lissoy, Ireland, the 'Auburn' of the poet, was knocked down by a cart, and afterwards removed bit by bit. It is said that some years previously, Dr Best, Bishop of Ardagh, thought of having it cut down: but on learning its poetical history, gave orders for its preservation.

Leaving now the historical associations of the hawthorn, we will glance at some of the popular traditions which have been associated with it. The reverence that was paid to it in medieval times, relics of which yet remain, especially in Brittany, was no doubt due to the popular belief that the Crown of Thorns was made from its branches. Sir John Maundeville (or Mandeville) says:

> The Jewes maden hym a croune of the braunches of Albespyne, that is whitethorne, and setten yt on hys heved. And therefore hath the whitethorn many virtues: for he that beareth a braunch on hym thereof, no thondre, ne no maner of tempest may dere [hurt] hym; ne in the hows that yt is ynne may non evil ghost entre.

We may trace the same belief in the virtues of the hawthorn down to later

'Llangollen Bridge' by John Alexander Gresse (1741-97); watercolour.
(*Victoria and Albert Museum, London; Crown copyright*)

times: thus Langham, in 1623, says 'the white thorne is never stricken with lightening'; and this is still the belief in Normandy. Scott gives, as an old superstition: 'To be delivered of witches, they hang in their entries haythorn, otherwise whitethorn, gathered on May-day.' In some parts of Ireland, as well as in France, the 'good people' are said to assemble in the branches, and hence, to pluck a leaf from a tree known to be visited by them is to incur their high displeasure. It may be from this or some kindred belief that it is, in some places, considered very unlucky to take May into the house: notably in Essex, where in our juvenile days we were well rated for so doing, in defiance of the 'manners and customs' of the district. Another French superstition is to the effect that the hawthorn utters groans and sighs upon the morning of Good Friday: while a modification of the tree-worship in old times still obtains in the department of Saone and Loire, if we may believe a French writer, who tells us that it is not rare to find in the spring a woman praying fervently before a hawthorn for the cure of her child, or some such blessing. Aubrey says that in Germany 'the common people also, the night before [May] day, fetch a certain thorn, and stick it at their house-door, believing the witches can then doe them no harm.'

The remedy which old Culpepper gives for the removing of a thorn may fairly come under the head of traditionary lore. He says that if cloths be wetted with the distilled juice of hawthorn flowers, and applied to any place where thorns abide in the flesh, 'it will notably draw them forth. And thus you see the thorne gives a medicine for its own pricking, and so doth almost everything else' – a paraphrase of the axiom of homeopathists, *similia similibus curantur*. Pepys, in his diary, gives two slightly differing versions of a wide-spread charm against a thorn, one of which runs:

Christ was of a Virgin born,
And he was pricked with a thorn;
And it did neither bell nor swell,
And I trust in Jesus this never will.

It was an old Suffolk farmhouse custom to give any servant, who could bring in a branch of hawthorn in full flower on May-day, a dish of cream for breakfast: but the change of style and consequent difficulty of finding the branch, has led to the disuse of the custom.

The weather proverbs in connection with the whitethorn are not very numerous. The Scotch proverb, 'Mony haws, mony snaws,' finds its counterpart in the generally-received notion that an abundance of fruit on the hawthorn betokens a severe winter. Another Scotch proverb is to the effect that 'harvest follows in thirteen weeks after the milk-white thorn scents the air'; and the French consider that its flowering is an infallible sign that the frosts of winter have come to an end.

Probably no tree adds so much to the beauty of our London parks during May and June as the hawthorn, both in its red and white varieties. Those in the Regent's Park are probably the same that are mentioned with admiration by Pepys. Jesse, in his 'Gleanings', has the following interesting passage on the remarkable old thorns in Bushy Park, from which it probably took its name. These trees are generally supposed to have been in existence at the time of Oliver Cromwell, the park being then used as a hare park. As they increase in age they have the property of separating themselves into different stems, some having four or five, or even six, which, as they separate, become regularly barked round, forming to appearance so many distinct trees closely planted together, except that they all meet at the butt of the tree. Some of the trees are now undergoing this process of separation, having already thrown out one stem, while in other parts they are deeply indented with seams down the whole stem. These, gradually deepening from opposite sides towards the centre, will at last split the tree into a number of separate stems which are barked round.

It appears, however, that this 'barking round' is not quite complete, as on the inner face of the stems is found, not bark, but the remains of the decayed heart-wood.

The names by which the whitethorn is known in different parts of the country are not very various, but some of them are interesting. Whitethorn itself is a name given to the tree from its light-coloured wood, in opposition to the Blackthorn or sloe. Although now confined to *Cratoegus*, it was formerly common to other trees; thus Sir John Maundeville speaks of the barberry as whitethorn. The name haw-thorn is simply the Saxon *hagadorn* or *hegedorn*, and corresponds with the German *hagedorn*, meaning hedge thorn. From this we may gather that the haw-thorn was employed from very early times in the making of our hedges (A-S *haga*, or *hege*); and possibly its general use for that purpose may have led to the application of the term *haga*, first to the shrub, and then to its fruit – haws being known as 'hagues' in the Lancashire district, where the tree itself is known as 'haythorn'. In Norfolk, a hedge is known as a 'hey'. Hagbush Lane, in the north of London, formerly a favourite resort of artists, and written of by Hone in the *Every Day Book*, means 'hawbush', or 'hawthorn bush' Lane. It has been urged, however, that instead of the name of the shrub having been taken from its place of growth, the reverse is the case: that *hoeg*, or *haga* being the name of the fruit, the tree bearing it would be called *hoegdorn*; and that being used in the making of fences, would give them the name of *haga* or *hoege*. The young plants of the hawthorn, when planted for hedges, are called quicks or quickset, quick being the A-S *cwic*, living (as occurring in the Anglican version of the Apostles' Creed), and quickset hedges being so called to distinguish them from fences made of dead wood. The name May, or May-bush, needs no explanation. Gerarde speaks of the latter as a London name. Parkinson tells us that a place near Nantwich, in Cheshire, was called White Greene, 'which tooke the name as it was thought from the white b shes of thornes which there they call greenes'. The young shoots are eaten by children throughout the country under the name of 'bread and cheese', and the fruits, generally known as haws, have, in Dorsetshire the pretty name of 'Pixie (*i.e.* fairy) Pears'.

Home Truths from Abroad

ANONYMOUS

'Oh! to be in England
Now that April's there,
And whoever wakes in England
Sees some morning in despair;
There's a horrible fog i' the heart of the town,
And the greasy pavement is damp and brown;
While the raindrop falls from the laden bough,
  In England now!

'And after April when May follows,'
How foolish seem the returning swallows.
Hark! how the east wind sweeps along the street,
And how we give one universal sneeze!
The hapless lambs at thought of mint sauce bleat,
And ducks are conscious of the coming peas.
Lest you should think the spring is really present,
A biting frost will come to make things pleasant,
And though the reckless flowers begin to blow,
They'd better far have nestled down below;
An English spring sets men and women frowning,
Despite the rhapsodies of Robert Browning.

'Rainy Day at Bisham' (1871) by Frederick Walker (1840-75); watercolour.
(*By courtesy of the Victoria and Albert Museum, London. Photograph: Brian Hunt; John R. Freeman & Co*)

Pleasant Sounds

BY JOHN CLARE (1793-1864)

Poetry came easily and naturally to John Clare,
the son of a cottage farmer, in spite of being
poorly educated. His first book of poetry,
published when he was twenty-seven, was an
enormous success, but interest in the 'peasant
poet' was short-lived and Clare ended his
days in a lunatic asylum

The rustling of leaves under the feet in woods and
under hedges;

The crumping of cat-ice and snow down wood-
rides, narrow lanes, and every street causeway;

Rustling through a wood or rather rushing, while
the wind halloos in the oak-top like thunder;

The rustle of birds' wings startled from their nests
or flying unseen into the bushes;

The whizzing of larger birds overhead in a wood,
such as crows, puddocks, buzzards;

The trample of robins and woodlarks on the brown
leaves, and the patter of squirrels on the green
moss;

The fall of an acorn on the ground, the pattering
of nuts on the hazel branches as they fall from
ripeness;

The flirt of the groundlark's wing from the
stubbles — how sweet such pictures on dewy
mornings, when the dew flashes from its brown
feathers!

Natural History by Train

This excerpt from *The Country-Side* **appeared in 1905. Today's** *Country-Side*, **published by The British Naturalists' Association (BENA), continues to provide its readers, every four months, with original observations on wild life and its protection**

ONE of the engine-drivers in the early days of railways has left it on record that the farmers used to bring their guns with them and from the roofless third-class carriages of the period shot at astonished birds during the slow journeys.

Birds are not astonished nowadays at trains. They appear to be as much at home on the railway as they would be in a quiet country lane. They use the hedges bordering the lines and the bushes on the embankments for nesting purposes, the road-bed ballast for dust baths, and the telegraph wires for perches.

I have several times seen even cuckoos stay on the wires within a few feet of trains rushing past, although they have been enveloped in steam for a few seconds. Indeed, the best and closest view I ever had of a cuckoo was last spring from the engine of a slow train, the bird being on a wire in a deep cutting showing not the least fear, although it was so close that I could have reached it with a walking-stick.

Rooks are fond of searching for bits of axle-grease which drop from passing trucks. Rats do the same and also lick the oil from points. Large numbers of these are killed, their heads being generally crushed by the wheels.

Fast trains take heavy toll of the wild life of the country. The front of the smoke-box, buffers, framing, etc, of an express engine will, after a long run on a fine summer day, be found nearly covered by winged insects, ranging in size from butterflies downwards, all stuck firmly to the part by which they were struck.

Often little bunches of feathers will be seen, which tell their own tale, and I have found small birds dead adhering to the oil and dirt of the wheels, brake rods, etc, after a long run.

Sometimes a bird will be caught by the exhaust steam from the chimney, and, if the engine is working heavily, will fall dead as though shot. I have seen numbers killed in this manner; even rooks; for, though the steam puffs look harmless enough, they are death-dealing to any bird caught by them within a foot or so above the chimney-top. Often a bird, in attempting to fly across the line in front of a train will realise the danger when just on the point of being struck, and turn on one side at a speed for fifty yards or so, too fast for the human eye to follow.

Among the many wild creatures I have known killed by trains have been a squirrel, a woodcock, two owls and a wryneck.

Birds will often fly alongside trains as though racing with them, but no bird appears to me to be able to fly over fifty miles an hour, and that only for short distances. Swifts and the swallow tribe are the fastest flyers, but these, when in a hurry, always fly in a zig-zag manner.

An Exciting Race

I was once firing on a night goods train, and just after daybreak, when running on a straight stretch of road at a speed of about twenty-two miles an hour, a fine hare suddenly appeared from the grass at the side of the track and started running along a narrow path near the outside rail in the same direction as the train.

With ears laid back, it appeared to be running at its utmost speed, and after going half a mile was about twenty yards ahead of the engine. After this it began to tire, and at a mile and a half

An English railway scene in 1855. (*Radio Times Hulton Picture Library*)

the engine had gradually gained until both were level. At this point the little path ended at the sloping end of a station platform, but instead of running up this the hare ran on between the rail and the brickwork of the platform, upon which, when nearly through the station, it attempted to jump, but failing to gain a foothold, fell back and was killed. It deserved a better fate.

There was nothing to prevent the hare turning back or running through the hedge and ending the race, but the path seemed to have a fascination for it.

Very few rabbits are killed by trains in comparison to the numbers which frequent the banks of the lines, as a rabbit when crossing a line invariably creeps under the rails instead of jumping over them.

Queer Nesting Places

No bird is more partial to the railway than the pied wagtail. Among the places I have known this bird to nest in are the following: a heap of scrap iron; a pile of sleepers; on the ground under a stack of rails weighing hundreds of tons slightly raised from the ground on timber; in a hollow place under a loose lump of chalk in a siding; and on the ballast under one of the rails of a branch-line over which eighteen trains ran daily.

During the week when I saw this nest the number of trains was increased to over thirty owing to a race-meeting on four days of that week, and the sitting bird had a very restless time, as whenever a train passed it flew from the nest, although it sat until the engine was running above it. I do not know if the wagtails succeeded in raising their young. They fully deserved to do so.

This elegant little bird is also fond of frequenting goods sidings to catch the flies about the trucks of stable manure and dust-bin refuse.

The Impudent Sparrow

No bird is so impudent as a London sparrow, and at a London suburban station the birds are often fed by enginemen. I was on an engine at this place eating some food and had forgotten the birds when I was surprised to see a hen sparrow perching on the handrail close to the cab window, while on the ground there were about twenty more waiting. As soon as the bird on the handrail saw that I had noticed it, it flew in onto the footplate within six inches of me, cocking its head on one side and looking up as though trying to remind me of my neglect. On my throwing some bread to the ground it quickly left the footplate for its share.

I once saw three sparrows which had been roosting inside the roof of an engine-shed fall to the floor suffocated by the smoke from an engine just below the birds. They had been gradually suffocated and had only lost foothold when nearly dead. They were as black as the smoke which killed them.

The telegraph wires above the platform of a station within six miles of Charing Cross have been used by a red-backed shrike for about ten weeks each summer for the last six summers. I have daily seen the male bird at the same spot looking like an overgrown sparrow, showing no fear of trains or the hundreds of passengers who use the platform.

Adlestrop

BY EDWARD THOMAS (1878-1917)

A poet and essayist, Edward Thomas was
killed in Flanders during the First World War.
His works show a keen observation of the
English pastoral scene

Yes. I remember Adlestrop —
The name, because one afternoon
Of heat the express train drew up there
Unwontedly. It was late June.

The steam hissed. Some one cleared his throat.
No one left and no one came
On the bare platform. What I saw
Was Adlestrop — only the name.

And willows, willow-herb, and grass,
And meadowsweet, and haycocks dry,
No whitless still and lonely fair
Than the high cloudlets in the sky.

And for that minute a blackbird sang
Close by, and round him, mistier,
Farther and farther, all the birds
Of Oxfordshire and Gloucestershire.

Happy Families

BY AUSTIN HATTON FROM THE *SUNDAY TELEGRAPH*, 2 JULY 1978

A WAGTAIL, piping overhead, insistently follows me as I walk, feeling guilty of trespass, along the river's bank, almost knee-deep at times in meadowsweet and willow-herb. It seems that I have interrupted the bird's efforts to instruct his young family in the art of catching flies in the reeds.

If only he can make noise enough while circling low over my head, the father seemingly believes that he can prevent my noticing his four little wagsters, sitting in drab obedience, in a splash of creeping jenny's old gold where the bank is smothered in the lowly plants of midsummer's riverside.

So, to humour him, I wander on, hard though it is to resist the temptation to take a closer look at his infants, already such a credit to him. Instead, I turn my attention to a wild duck and her mallard husband, piqued by the furtive manner in which they are paddling idly around in the shallows.

Then I realise that the wild duck is softly warning infants on the bank to stay out of sight until she can, hoping not to make it too obvious, join them in the loosestrife. Again, so it seems, I am upsetting a family outing.

It is, indeed, difficult to know which way to turn. In the hedgerow, a pair of young goldfinches, in fawns and buffs led by a scarlet-capped parent, whirl away on flickering gold and black wings, their twittering music plainly indicating that the little family resented being rudely disturbed.

Farther along the lane that leads away from the river a shrike is standing on the top bar of a field gate, so busy with a black bumble bee that he virtually ignores me. With parental solicitude, he 'tops and tails' the dead insect and carves up the middle part for his two sparrow-like fledglings.

Only an occasional warning in harsh tones suggests that the shrike, his black eye-stripes and raptor's beak making him look anything but a doting parent, realises the vulnerability of his progeny cringing on the warm wood of the farm gate.

But, in contrast, two whitethroats, confused because I have unwittingly come face to face with their three fledglings, cry their fear to the whole hedgerow by uttering in a duet of despair the hoarse croaks of practised tragedians. And to add to the commotion they jump about from twig to twig.

Such a brouhaha can only attract the attention of those who are quick to take advantage of such a situation. To relax the tension I move away, dreading any fresh involvement in family affairs.

Woodcock and family, an illustration from John Gould's *Birds of Great Britain* (1862-93). (*Fotomas Index*)

Wild Flowers

BY RICHARD JEFFERIES (1848-87)

Richard Jefferies was a field naturalist who had poetic perceptions. This is an extract from *The Open Air*, one of his books on the English fields, woods and hedgerows, and the people inhabiting the countryside

A FRIEND said, 'Why do you go the same road every day? Why not have a change and walk somewhere else sometimes? Why keep on up and down the same place?' I could not answer; till then it had not occurred to me that I did always go one way; as for the reason of it I could not tell; I continued in my old mind while the summers went away. Not till years afterwards was I able to see why I went the same round and did not care for change. I do not want change: I want the same old and loved things, the same wild flowers, the same trees and soft ash-green; the turtle-doves, the blackbirds, the coloured yellowhammer sing, sing, singing so long as there is light to cast a shadow on the dial, for such is the measure of his song, and I want them in the same place. Let me find them morning after morning,

43

the starry-white petals radiating, striving upwards to their ideal. Let me see the idle shadows resting on the white dust; let me hear the humble-bees, and stay to look down on the rich dandelion disk. Let me see the very thistles opening their great crowns – I should miss the thistles; the reed-grasses hiding the moorhen; the bryony bine, at first crudely ambitious and lifted by force of youthful sap straight above the hedgerow to sink of its own weight presently and progress with crafty tendrils; swifts shot through the air with outstretched wings like crescent-headed shaftless arrows darted from the clouds; the chaffinch with a feather in her bill; all the living staircase of the spring, step by step, upwards to the great gallery of the summer – let me watch the same succession year by year.

Why, I knew the very dates of them all – the reddening elm, the arum, the hawthorn leaf, the celandine, the may; the yellow iris of the waters, the heath of the hillside. The time of the nightingale – the place to hear the first note; onwards to the drooping fern and the time of the redwing – the place of *his* first note, so welcome to the sportsman as the acorn ripens and the pheasant, come to the age of manhood, feeds himself; onwards to the shadow-less days – the long shadowless winter, for in winter it is the shadows we miss as much as the light. They lie over the summer sward, design upon design, dark lace on green and gold; they glorify the sunlight: they repose on the distant hills like gods upon Olympus; without shadow, what even is the sun? At the foot of the great cliffs by the sea you may know this, it is dry glare; mighty ocean is dearer as the shadows of the clouds sweep over as they sweep over the green corn. Past the shadowless winter, when it is all shade, and therefore no shadow; onwards to the first coltsfoot and on to the seed-time again; I knew the dates of all of them. I did not want change; I wanted the

same flowers to return on the same day, the titlark to rise soaring from the same oak to fetch down love with a song from heaven to his mate on the nest beneath. No change, no new thing; if I found a fresh wildflower in a fresh place, still it wove at once into the old garland. In vain, the very next year was different even in the same place – *that* had been a year of rain, and the flag-flowers were wonderful to see; *this* was a dry year, and the flags not half the height, the gold of the flower not so deep; next year the fatal billhook came and swept away a slow-grown hedge that had given me crab-blossom in cuckoo-time and hazelnuts in harvest. Never again the same, even in the same place.

A little feather droops downwards to the ground – a swallow's feather fuller of miracle than the Pentateuch – how shall that feather be placed again in the breast where it grew? Nothing twice. Time changes the places that knew us, and if we go back in afteryears, still even then it is not the old spot; the gate swings differently, new thatch has been put on the old gables, the road has been widened, and the sward the driven sheep lingered on is gone. Who dares to think then? For faces fade as flowers, and there is no consolation. So now I am sure I was right in always walking the same way by the starry flowers striving upwards on a slender ancestry of stem; I would follow the plain old road today if I could. Let change be far from me; that irresistible change must come is bitter indeed. Give me the old road, the same flowers – they were only stitchwort – the old succession of days and garland, ever weaving into it fresh wildflowers from far and near. Fetch them from distant mountains, discover them on decaying walls, in unsuspected corners; though never seen before, still they are the same: there has been a place in the heart waiting for them.

'Alderney Cows and Calves' (1820) by Robert Hills (1769-1844); watercolour.
(*By courtesy of the Victoria and Albert Museum, London. Photograph: Brian Hunt; John R. Freeman & Co*)

Milking Time

FROM *TESS OF THE D'URBERVILLES*, 1891 BY THOMAS HARDY (1840-1928)

THE red and white herd nearest at hand, which had been phlegmatically waiting for the call, now trooped towards the steading in the background, their great bags of milk swinging under them as they walked. Tess followed slowly in their rear, and entered the barton by the open gate through which they had entered before her. Long thatched sheds stretched round the enclosure, their slopes encrusted with vivid green moss, and their eaves supported

A milkman watches a country woman using a hand-churn, widely used for butter-making at home at the time of this photograph (1857). From *Grundy's English Views*.
(*Radio Times Hulton Picture Library*)

by wooden posts rubbed to a glossy smoothness by the flanks of infinite cows and calves of bygone years, now passed to an oblivion almost inconceivable in its profundity. Between the posts were ranged the milchers, each exhibiting herself at the present moment to a whimsical eye in the rear as a circle on two stalks, down the centre of which a switch moved pendulum-wise; while the sun, lowering itself behind this patient row, threw their shadows accurately inwards upon the wall. Thus it threw shadows of these obscure and homely figures every evening with as much care over each contour as if it had been the profile of a Court beauty on a palace wall; copied them as diligently as it had copied Olympian shapes on marble façades long ago, or the outline of Alexander, Caesar, and the Pharaohs . . .

When skimming was done – which as the milk diminished with the approach of autumn, was a lessening process day by day – Retty and the rest went out. The lovers followed them.

'Our tremulous lives are so different from theirs, are they not?' Clare musingly observed to her, as he regarded the three figures tripping before him through the frigid pallor of opening day.

'Not so very different, I think,' she said.

'Why do you think that?'

'There be very few women's lives that are not – tremulous,' Tess replied, pausing over the new word as if it impressed her.

Buttercups

BY PETER JONES (born 1929)

Peter Jones is both a poet and a literary
critic. This poem and 'The Heron' were first
published in a collection, *Rain,* in 1969

Such meditations
of the yellow sun in the grass —

so many dawns in the field.

All midsummer
in one flower —

And so much gold!

A Talk with a Country Vicar

BY W. H. HUDSON (1841-1922)

Published in 1909, William Henry Hudson's book *Afoot in England* **contains the following amusing extract, which tells how the naturalist author, whilst on a cycling tour, stopped at an enchanting village on the Devon-Cornwall border . . .**

NEVER, I thought, had I seen a lovelier village, with its old picturesque cottages shaded by ancient oaks and elms, and the great church with its stately tower looking dark against the luminous western sky. Dismounting again I stood for some time admiring the scene, wishing that I could make that village my home for the rest of my life, conscious at the same time that it was the mood, the season, the magical hour, which made it seem so enchanting. Presently a young man, the first human figure that presented itself to my sight, appeared, mounted on a big cart-horse and leading a second horse by a halter, and rode down into the pool to bathe the animals' legs and give them a drink. He was a sturdy-looking young fellow with a sun-browned face, in earth-coloured, working clothes, with a small cap stuck on the back of his round curly head; he probably imagined himself not a bad-looking young man, for while his horses were drinking he laid over on the broad bare back and bending down studied his own reflection in the bright water. Then an old woman came out of a cottage close by, and began talking to him in her West Country dialect in a thin high-pitched cracked voice. Their talking was the only sound in the village; so silent was it that all the rest of its inhabitants might have been in bed and fast asleep; then, the conversation ended, the young man rode out with a great splashing and the old woman turned into her cottage again, and I was left in solitude.

Still I lingered: I could not go just yet; the chances were that I should never again see that sweet village in that beautiful aspect at the twilight hour. For now it came into my mind that I could not very well settle there for the rest of my life; I could not, in fact, tie myself to any place without sacrificing certain other advantages I possessed; and the main thing was that by taking root I should deprive myself of the chance of looking on still other beautiful scenes and experiencing other sweet surprises. I was wishing that I had come a little earlier on the scene to have had time to borrow the key of the church and get a sight of the interior, when all at once I heard a shrill voice and a boy appeared running across the wide green space of the churchyard. A second boy followed, then another, then still others, and I saw that they were going into the church by the side door. They were choirboys going to practice. The church was open then, and late as it was I could have half an hour inside before it was dark! The stream was spanned by an old stone bridge above the ford, and going over it I at once made my way to the great building, but even before entering it I discovered that it possessed an organ of extraordinary power and that someone was performing on it with a vengeance. Inside the noise was tremendous – a bigger noise from an organ, it seemed to me, than I had ever heard before, even at the Albert Hall and the Crystal Palace; but even more astonishing than the uproar was the sight that met my eyes. The boys, nine or ten sturdy little rustics with round sunburnt West Country faces, were playing the roughest game ever witnessed in a church. Some were engaged in a sort of flying fight, madly pursuing one another up and down the aisles and over the pews, and whenever one overtook another he would seize hold of him and they would struggle together until one was thrown and received a vigorous pommelling. Those who were not fighting were dancing to the music. It was great fun to them, and they were shouting and laughing their loudest, only not a sound of it all could be heard on account of the thunderous roar of the organ which filled and seemed to make the whole building tremble. The boys took no notice of me, and seeing that there was a singularly fine west window, I went to it and stood there some time with my back to the game which was going on at the other end of the building, admiring the beautiful colours and trying to make out the subjects depicted. In the centre part, lit by the afterglow in the sky to a wonderful brilliance, was the figure of a saint, a lovely young woman in a blue robe with an abundance of loose golden-red hair, and an aureole about her head. Her pale face wore a sweet and placid expression, and her eyes, of a pure forget-me-not blue, were looking straight into mine. As I stood there the music, or noise, ceased and a very profound silence followed – not a giggle, not a whisper from the outrageous young barbarians, and not a sound of the organist or of any one speaking to them. Presently I became conscious of some person standing almost but not quite abreast of me, and turning sharply I found a clergyman at my side. He was the vicar, the person who had been letting himself go on the organ; a slight man with a handsome, pale, ascetic face, clean-shaven, very dark-eyed, looking more like an Italian monk or priest than an English clergyman. But although rigidly ecclesiastic in his appearance and dress, there was something curiously engaging in him, along with a subtle look which it was not easy to fathom. There was a light in his dark eyes which reminded me of a flame seen through a smoked glass or a thin black veil, and a slight restless movement about the corners of his mouth as if a smile was just on the point of breaking out. But it never quite came; he kept his gravity even when he said things which would have gone very well with a smile.

51

'A Village Choir' (exhibited 1847) by Thomas Webster (1800-86); oils.
(*Victoria and Albert Museum, London; Crown copyright*)

'I see,' he spoke, and his penetrating musical voice had, too, like his eyes and mouth, an expression of mystery in it, 'that you are admiring our beautiful west window, especially the figure in the centre. It is quite new – everything is new here – the church itself was only built a few years ago. This window is its chief glory: it was done by a good artist – he has done some of the most admired windows of recent years; and the centre figure is supposed to be a portrait of our generous patroness. At all events she sat for it to him. You have probably heard of Lady Y——?'

'What!' I exclaimed. 'Lady Y——: that funny old woman!'

'No – middle-aged,' he corrected, a little frigidly and perhaps a little mockingly at the same time.

'Very well, middle-aged if you like; I don't know her personally. One hears about her; but I did not know she had a place in these parts.'

'She owns most of this parish and has done so much for us that we can very well look leniently on a little weakness – her wish that the future inhabitants of the place shall not remember her as a middle-aged woman not remarkable for good looks – "funny", as you just now said.'

He was wonderfully candid, I thought. But what extraordinary benefits had she bestowed on them, I asked, to enable them to regard, or to say, that this picture of a very beautiful young female was her likeness?

'Why,' he said, 'the church would not have been built but for her. We were astonished at the sum she offered to contribute towards the work, and at once set about pulling the small old church down so as to rebuild on the exact site.'

'Do you know,' I returned, 'I can't help saying something you will not like to hear. It is a very fine church, no doubt, but it always angers me to hear of a case like this where some ancient church is pulled down and a grand new one raised in its place to the honour and glory of some rich parvenu with or without a brand-new title.'

'You are not hurting me in the least,' he replied, with that change which came from time to time in his eyes as if the flame behind the screen had suddenly grown brighter. 'I agree with every word you say; the meanest church in the land should be cherished as long as it will hold together. But unfortunately ours had to come down. It was very old and decayed past mending. The floor was six feet below the level of the surrounding ground and frightfully damp. It had been examined over and over again by experts during the past forty or fifty years, and from the first they pronounced it a hopeless case, so that it was never restored. The interior, right down to the time of demolition, was like that of most country churches of a century ago, with the old black worm-eaten pews, in which the worshippers shut themselves up as if in their own houses or castles. On account of the damp we were haunted by toads. You smile, sir, but it was no smiling matter for me during my first year as vicar, when I discovered that it was the custom here to keep pet toads in the church. It sounds strange and funny, no doubt, but it is a fact that all the best people in the parish had one of these creatures, and it was customary for the ladies to bring it a weekly supply of provisions – bits of meat, hard-boiled eggs chopped up, and earthworms, and whatever else they fancied it would like –

Our Church; an engraving by Frank Carless for *The Quiver*, 1874. (*The British Library, London*)

in their reticules. The toads, I suppose,  knew when it was Sunday – their feeding day; at all events they would crawl out of their holes in the floor under the pews to receive their rations – and caresses. The toads got on my nerves with rather unpleasant consequences. I preached in a way which my listeners did not appreciate or properly understand, particularly when I took for my subject our duty towards the lower animals, including reptiles.'

'Batrachians,' I interposed, echoing as well as I could the tone in which he had rebuked me before.

'Very well, batrachians – I am not a naturalist. But the impression created on their minds appeared to be that I was rather an odd person in the pulpit. When the time came to pull the old church down the toad-keepers were bidden to remove their pets, which they did with considerable reluctance. What became of them I do not know – I never inquired. I used to have a careful inspection made of the floor to make sure that these creatures were not put back in the new building, and I am happy to think it is not suited to their habits. The floors are very well cemented, and are dry and clean.'

Having finished his story he invited me to go to the parsonage and get some refreshment. 'I dare say you are thirsty,' he said.

But it was getting late; it was almost dark in the church by now, although the figure of the golden-haired saint still glowed in the window and gazed at us out of her blue eyes.

'I must not waste more of your time,' I added. 'There are your boys still patiently waiting to begin their practice – such nice quiet little fellows!'

'Yes, they are,' he returned a little bitterly, a sudden accent of weariness in his voice and no trace now of what I had seen in his countenance a little while ago – the light that shone and brightened behind the dark eye and the little play about the corners of the mouth, as of dimpling motions on the surface of a pool.

The Miller

BY JOHN CUNNINGHAM (1729-73)

The following poem appeared in *The Universal Magazine* in 1760. Cunningham wrote much contemplative verse, some of which was included in his *Poems, Chiefly Pastoral* (1766)

In a plain pleasant cottage, conveniently neat,
With a mill and some meadows – a freehold
   estate,
A well-meaning miller by labour supplies
Those blessings that grandeur to great ones denies:

No passions to plague him, no cares to torment,
His constant companions are health and content;
Their lordships in lace may remark if they will,
He's honest tho' doub'd with the dust of his mill.

   Ere the lark's early carrols salute the new day
He springs from his cottage as jocund as May;
He cheerfully whistles, regardless of care,
Or sings the last ballad he bought at the fair:

While courtiers are toil'd in the cobwebs of state,
Or bribing elections in hopes to be great,
No fraud, or ambition his bosom does fill,
Contented he works, if there's grist for his mill.

   On Sunday bedeck'd in his homespun array,
At church he's the loudest, to chaunt or to pray:
He sits to a dinner of plain English food,
Tho' simple the pudding, his appetite's good;

At night, when the priest and exciseman are gone,
He quaffs at the alehouse with Roger and John,
The reels to his pillow, and dreams of no ill;
No monarch more blest than the man of the mill.

'The Tyne from Windmill Hill, Gateshead' (c 1825) by Thomas Miles
Richardson Snr (1784-1848); oils.
(*Laing Art Gallery, Tyne and Wear County Museums Service*)

Farnham Fairs

BY GEORGE STURT (1863-1927)

Taken from *A Small Boy in the Sixties*, **this is an account of fairtime at a country town by a great writer (also known as George Bourne) whose descriptions of rural life rank with the earlier authors Cobbett and Jefferies**

IN my childhood Farnham had three fairs during the year. The first may have been originally a religious occasion, for it was held on Ascension Day, but it was afterwards fixed for May 10th. Midsummer Day was the date for the second; and the third was on the 13th – afterwards changed to the 10th – of November. I don't know whether the incidence of the second on St John's Day had anything to do with the matter, but the Midsummer Fair was commonly called a Pleasure Fair, as if to contrast it against the others, though they all alike seemed to me opportunities for shouting men to drive horses, cattle, and especially sheep. Occasionally some strange wild-looking man would come into the town with sheep – some shepherd not used to streets at all, but only at home on a lonely down, where he never saw or was seen by anybody but his flock and his dog. Perhaps not in those far-off days (though one never knows) but in after years there would fall on me amidst the hubbub and stench of the thronged fair, an influence from the shy wild look of a stranger, as if he had brought with him views of blue horizons and bleak wide skies.

Fair Day was a holiday at all the Farnham schools; farmers wanted to see their sons from the Grammar School or Poppleton's, their daughters from Miss Stratford's; and of course the shopkeepers (by no means 'superior' persons or 'highbrows' then) had to observe the day. Whether the Fair began overnight I cannot now remember. By the time I was a young man mumpers from all the neighbourhood – having waited in the near lanes for hours – would come hurrying in to the town on the previous evening at the stroke of six (church bell or town hall clock), and stake out their 'standings' in Castle Street. But at any rate in my earliest years the Fair was already in full blast o'mornings when I woke up for the day. Already could be heard unwonted noises from down in the street; and one had not to look long to see down below a hurry of strange sights – a herd of black Welsh bullocks coming over from Blackwater Fair, a dishevelled gang of gypsies, a flock of sheep thronging the street from

Fair Day at Farnham, about the turn of the century. (*Surrey County Library, Farnham, Surrey*)

side to side, sheep dogs rushing and barking to keep slow sheep on the move and in order, a little group of farmers (not, as on market days, in their best clothes), a show cart, a dirty gig or two, unkempt mumpers quarrelling and spoiling for a fight at public house doors, hard-faced travelling women with sticky-looking brown hair; and at times, as if all this straggling, careless, swearing, jostling crowd were not enough, along the street would come yelling, while the road was just cleared and no more by folk who gave no other heed, a shady-looking fellow – a horse coper – running a frightened horse for sale. No other heed? Not quite so, either. Anybody with a whip – and there were many, gyp, farmer, half-and-half – was liable to crack it loudly, for the fun of frightening the horse into a faster trot. And above the yells, the bleatings, the clatter of horse-hooves, and loud chatter and other nameless noises, came the thin toot of toy trumpets bought at a stall, the cries of showmen, the bang of beetle, driving into the road the stakes for some 'cokernut'-shy or still unfinished stall. Guns popped

59

at shooting-galleries; children squalled; oh! there wasn't half a din!

Of course one had to hurry out to see the fun; yet the racket in the usually staid street was almost alarming. Fortunately there were hands ('puddies') of rather braver people – a brother, and, bigger still, a sister – to hold on to. Thus fortified one could visit the nearer stalls – first Bonny Rogers's year after year in flies. Yet, as we never bought them at any other time, they were a sign of Fair Day, and I ate them. Round the corner from the Borough three or four more stalls stretched up Castle Street. Big coarse 'sugar-sticks', 'hundreds and thousands', 'hard-bake', could be had at one stall, china dogs and no doubt other shiny crockery-ware things at another.

Beyond came a dingy medley; a

'Fairlop Oak and Fair' (1774) by Samuel Hieronymous Grimm (1733-94); watercolour. (*By courtesy of the Victoria and Albert Museum, London. Photograph: Brian Hunt; John R. Freeman & Co*)

the Borough, opposite The Queen's Head. There it was customary to buy gingerbread – thick hunks made for the Fair, or circular disks embellished with lemon peel which had to be removed. Hunks or disks, it was none of it really nice – gingerbread a trifle bitter even – yet the occasion made it palatable. And that was the case when, hurrying to a quiet back street, we added to our gingerbread a supply of 'Garibaldi' biscuits. Even then I almost disliked 'Garibaldis' – so chucky and tough, looking like baked swinging-boat or two – already full of louts and squeaking hoydens – and swinging so far across the pavement that you couldn't pass safely without hugging close in to the houses; a popping shooting-gallery; a man supplying a saucer of whelks (vinegar and pepper too, of course) to some pleased-looking villager; and in and out, everywhere, a shabby tangle of shabby people not knowing how to be idle, yet bent on doing nothing but be amused for once.

Soon, fifty yards or so farther on, the

'The Road to Fairlop Fair' (1818) by Thomas Rowlandson (1756-1827); ink and watercolour wash. (*By courtesey of the Victoria and Albert Museum, London. Photograph: Brian Hunt; John R. Freeman & Co*)

sheep-pens began; and these stretched all up Castle Street on one side and round the corner out of sight – a furlong or so of pens of huddling and bleating sheep. Probably the sheep were frightened; but they could not run away. One could look (not being very tall oneself) into their silly eyes; with a stick (and every boy who was a boy had to have a stick on Fair Day – not a finicking cane or dandified stick either, but a useful thing, ash or nut or withy, cut from a hedge, like a farmer's) – with it one could poke into any sheep's fleece at pleasure, not to learn anything about the animal, but because that was the thing to do. Were not other boys and men at it? All up and down the pavement, and in the roadway beyond the narrow line of sheep, people were wandering – or some were sitting on the hurdles which made the sides of the pens. The people may have been farmers at business, or drovers, or idlers; but it was the thing to tickle your stick into the close South Down wool, and no sheep could prevent you.

Across the street (I seldom went that side) were first, I think, a few pigpens; but, even before the turn at the upper end of the street was reached, little groups could be seen of scared cows and heifers. These were not penned in; but each group was kept from straying by a man or two with a stick, willing enough to whack back into place any weary or uneasy beast that tried to get away. Round the corner – right away past Castle Steps and even up to The Grange – the road for a quarter of a mile was thick with cattle of all sorts. There probably was no great danger there, but I can only remember seeing it once. It was truly no place for a little boy.

Towards dinnertime the Borough and West Street for fifty yards or so, today alive with motor cars, began to fill up with rows of horses. They stood with their tails towards the pavement, facing towards the street they half blocked; and though they stood patient enough, it was not altogether pleasant on the thronged pavement, behind their flicking tails and stamping hooves. Besides, the men who gathered about these horses were a sinister-looking lot, cunning, shifty of eye, loud of speech. I avoided the horses even more timidly than I avoided the cattle. And perhaps there was reason for this too. For it was terrible to see a horse 'running', to hear the owner who held the halter keeping up his hullaballoo all through the swaying crowds in the street. It may have been fun to others; it seemed death to me. The horses were often tied together in groups, and not a few of the groups were New Forest Ponies. Harness there was none; but in many cases bright yellow straw had been knotted into tail or mane.

As the day wore on and the cattle and sheep and horses disappeared, Castle Street filled up more and more with 'shows' and lounging villagers bent on pleasure. I think the cokernut-shy had not quite ousted the more ancient Aunt Sally; certainly not wooden balls but thick sticks about eighteen inches long were the missiles. They were usually thrown whirling from one end, but one clever man tossed his sticks level from the middle and won too many cokernuts. There was a rich selection of fat ladies, bearded ladies, abortions of all sorts. Some of the shows were fronted with platforms with steps up to them, where mountebanks could address the public – 'Walk up! Walk up! Ladies and Gentlemen,' or musicians could deafen them with trumpet and drum; and many shows were alluring with gaudy paintings on the outside – Royal Bengal Tigers, Kings, Slaves – I cannot recall what. For I went into none of these shows though I would have liked to go. Not once could any of the seniors with me be persuaded to venture on...

But two or three minor shows I did get into; and I can still conjure up a recollection of grey-looking damp-looking canvas for their tents. In one of them you did but walk round, putting one eye to a hole, through which a view could be seen. It was a dismal show – as cheerful as squinting into a tiny microscope let into the end of a pen-holder and seeing perhaps Windsor Castle or The Crystal Palace – a wonder we sometimes failed to wonder at. In this gloomy 'peep-show' of Farnham Fair might be seen 'The Relief of Lucknow', or 'The Coronation of Queen Victoria' or some other equally exciting spectacle. There were but nine or ten peep-holes in all . . .

In the late afternoon it became possible to buy little penny squirts – forerunners of 'ladies' tormentors'; though hardly so far off may one date the cry 'All the fun of the fair!' Late in the afternoon too, while the throngs of people thickened, the roundabouts began to be busy. I never rode on one. In fact, about teatime I seem to have forsaken the Fair and gone home; for no memory remains of any evening there. Once, a chimney afire at home raised a cry in the Fair that Sturt's newspaper shop was afire, and brought hopeful people crowding to see; occasionally a loud bang told where some wag had thrown a squib down into the crowd. But this I never saw. And if I saw, I no-wise remember, any of my father's cronies or customers, any farmer friends, dropping in for a smoke on Fair Day evening, as doubtless they did. Doubtless too I had myself been packed off to bed betimes. The next morning, unless for filth I didn't see, or possibly piles of hurdles from the dismantled pens I didn't notice, nothing was left of the Fair but a smell, mostly of sheep, that clung to the ancient street for a few hours. The quiet of the centuries was recovered. From aloft the Castle looked down as it had done in all my memory, upon a very peaceful town.

Nettleworth Horse and Foal Show

BY FRED KITCHEN (1890-1969)

The following episode, derived from *Nettleworth Parva*, is based on the memories of the Derbyshire-born author, who started life as a ploughman in the early days of this century. Nettleworth Parva is a purely fictional hamlet, but the local characters he describes, and their ways, are very typical of the period

THE most keenly awaited event in agricultural circles was the Nettleworth Horse and Foal Show, held in Magna Park on the August Bank Holiday Monday. There were always some good entries from the Parva farms, but this year the stock on show seemed better than ever. George Western's mare Ruby had borne a splendid colt foal with good knees and hocks, and wide-chested and dark brown like its dam, which looked a prize winner. Ralph was showing in the class for the best matched plough team, with two perfectly matched dappled greys out of Flower, the grey mare. Farmer Robinson was again there with his hunter mare Vashti with foal at foot.

In the show-field on the auspicious day stood a long line of horses of all breeds in their canvas stalls, excitement in the flash of their eyes at the unaccustomed noise and bustle, and the music of the band engaged to brighten up the proceedings. First in the line came the Hunter Class, some with their foals, some waiting to be ridden in their entry class. Then the Hackneys, those proud conceited animals that came somewhere between the pony and the cart-horse. Their watchword was 'action', and they stepped around the ring showing their paces, drawing a queer four-wheeled contraption, known as a 'sulky', of no material benefit, except to be drawn around a show-ring. The largest entries were in the Shire Class, for in spite of the internal combustion engine and the steam-driven truck the draught horse was still the country's main motive power.

Horse dealers, wearing stiff, uncomfortable, starched collars, and even stiffer and more uncomfortable breeches and gaiters of white whipcord, hovered around the three- and four-year-olds, hoping to bring about a sale for some

'Mares and Foals in a Landscape' (c 1760-70) by George Stubbs (1724-1806); oils.
(*The Tate Gallery, London*)

The Bay Pony; wood engraving by Thomas Bewick (1753-1823). (*Fotomas Index*)

prospective customer, who would condemn the proud colt to doing a daily round of the city streets until its feet became ruined with treading the granite sets – never more would it stand on its hind legs to give battle with its forefront as in its pride and glory of this present afternoon. Parva brought home its share of the honours. George Western's mare Ruby, with foal at foot, was judged the best mare with foal in the field, while Ralph, with his pair of greys, easily outpaced all other entries. Robinson's Vashti again came first for mares in the Hunter Class with foal at foot.

Another interesting class was for the best-groomed cart-horse. One felt sorry for the entrant that didn't get a prize, for grooming a cart-horse, and cleaning the harness to pass judgement under the scrutiny of the judge, takes weeks of toil and labour. Every buckle and strap is tested as to its ease or difficulty in being unfastened, every chink and crease in the leather is searched for a speck of dust, and finally the horse's harness is taken off while with a silk handkerchief the judge calmly wipes the horse's flank to see if perchance a speck of dust adheres to the silk. After which the carter may reclothe his steed in all its finery – brasses, bells, martingales, hip-straps and all its bravery of rosettes and caddis – while within his heart is a sinking feeling that he hasn't quite brought it off.

The tradesman's turn-out is not quite so exactingly scrutinised. The action of the horse is taken into account, perhaps even more than the originality and suitability of the vehicle to the particular tradesman, but be it butcher, baker or candlestick-maker, the tradesman's turn-out makes a colourful event in the afternoon's performance.

There were pony races; there was 'Tilting at the Ring', with hunters and hacks; there was a large beer booth and a small tent where one could get tea or lemonade, and moreover there was a prize brass band playing overtures and serenades until dusk of evening, so that he must have been a sour-bellied curmudgeon who said he hadn't had his shilling's worth, which was the price of entry at the gate.

At 4 p.m. the competitors were allowed to take their chargers out of the showground, and a happy cavalcade might have been seen descending Magna hill, bringing home the honours.

It was a warm evening of golden sunshine, and the hut and the Green were forsaken, for most of the young folk were up at Magna finishing off show-day by riding on the dobby horses and the swings, whose steam organ had been blaring out 'Yip-i-addy-I-ay' ever since mid-morning. George Western, Frank Smith and Jon Keppel were reclining at ease in the shade of the hut discussing the affairs of the day. There was not a cloud in the sky and the only movable object on the horizon was a boy on a bicycle careering wildly down Magna hill with his feet on the foot-rests.

'Yon youth'll break his flipping neck,' commented George, adding, 'And that'll leave more bread for them 'ats in need.'

No one heeded George's laconic statement and the boy, then entering the village, reared his bike on the causeway edge and lustily bawled out, 'England declares war on Germany! Special edition! England declares war on Germany!'

The storm had broken: 4th August 1914.

The Cyclist

BY DENIS CURLING (1921-42)

This verse, and 'Winter', hitherto published
privately, were written by Denis Curling just
before the Second World War, during which he
served as a fighter-pilot and was killed in
action over northern France

The road is climbing now between the stately
   pines
To drop abruptly from my view;
Beyond, the valley into which the hill inclines,
A chequered floor of shadows, shapes and lines,
Fades in the distance to the cloudless blue.

Here now I hang upon the summit of the hill,
Poised as an eagle for a dive.
For one brief moment all the air is still,
And then great gusts sweep through my hair and
   fill
My lungs, as pedals answer to the drive.

The road, the bushes and the trees appear to glide
While I have merged into my steed,
And, as an anchored ship mounts over waves and
   tide,
So do I now as on a current ride,
And all my frame thrills to the song of speed.

This lady cyclist, c 1902, can look forward to a pleasant ride, unhindered by motor traffic, with her photographer-companion. (*Kodak Museum, Harrow*)

A jolly cycling party, c 1906. Presumably they are at the outset of their journey, having just arrived by train. (*Kodak Museum, Harrow*)

Motor Notes

BY A ROADSIDE NATURALIST

Back in the summer of 1907, when motoring along the lanes was still a pleasure, *The Country-Side* published these rural observations and suggestions for drivers in the magazine's series entitled 'Motor Notes'

FOR the purposes of observation, the motor car has much of the advantage which came to the first bicyclists. It was my fortune to do a good deal of motoring in what were fairly early days – in the summers of 1900 and 1901 – when I became familiar not only with the better known parts of England, but also with some of the less accessible regions of Yorkshire and Cornwall and Monmouthshire, and one of the great delights of motoring then was the way in which one was constantly taking nature by surprise. The wild things had not begun to learn to get out of the way of a car, and it astounded me to discover how full of stoats and weasels are our country roads. Once we ran over a stoat; several times we came across them when they had just killed a rabbit on the high road and had no time to drag the victim into the cover of the ditch. Every day we saw them trotting along by the hedge-sides, into which, in their bewilderment at the awful new phenomenon, they had no time to scramble before the car was abreast of them. The number of hedgehogs, too, which used to come out in the evening, apparently for the express purpose of being run over (and hedgehog spines are not good for motor tyres), was a constant surprise, I had no idea that there were so many hedgehogs in England as we used to see then.

Fortunately, animals soon learn to accommodate themselves to new and dangerous conditions. In those days almost every horse which one met on a country road tried to bolt at sight of the car, and a large part of the motorist's time was spent in getting out and helping to lead refractory beasts past the new terror in the road. With the number of cars that are running now, if horses were as afraid of them today as they used to be seven years ago, riding or driving on the high roads would be almost an impossibility. And wild animals have been nearly as quick to change their habits to conform to the

An afternoon siesta for the passengers while the driver tinkers with the engine of a 1904 Fiat. (*Radio Times Hulton Picture Library*)

new conditions. One may run all day now on any of the great main roads, and see no more stoats or weasels or hedgehogs than you will see on foot. On less frequented ways the mere rapidity of approach still brings you once in a while into the middle of domestic scenes which are by no means intended for human inspection. Almost the last time that I was out, a sparrow-hawk struck a lark as it was crossing the road a hundred yards or so ahead of us, and we were on it so much sooner than it expected, that to this minute I do not know how the hawk managed to rise as it did from under our front wheel without being hit.

If you expect to see much of nature on the road, however, you must not care about speed records, and, personally, I have got past that stage in driving when speed appealed to me. Not all motorists will agree with me, but those who do will be the wise ones, and those of most experience, when I say that as a general rule twenty miles an hour is fast enough. Above that speed one sees nothing of the country through which one passes, except only in the broadest outline; below that speed one can see almost everything. The motion is so much smoother and one is so much nearer the ground, that, in my opinion, you see more of the details of the country – more of nature – when running at eighteen miles in a car than you can at eight in a dog cart.

A car is used by different owners in three distinct ways. To some it is merely a machine for getting from place to place, in which aspect it is just as well to have high speed at command in case of need. To others, and this is how most novices regard it, it is a way of getting excitement – of enjoying the thrills of rapid movement, for which, of course, speed becomes the chief essential. But the rational use of the car, and that for which a constantly increasing number of motorists are coming to love it, is to travel at such a speed that one has all the joys of a motion faster than one can experience either on a bicycle or behind a horse, without sacrificing the delight of seeing the country as you go by. To 'let her out' now and again when you have a flat stretch of dull road ahead of you, and no chance of inconveniencing or endangering other users of the highway, that is human and excusable; but the man who systematically exceeds the speed limit is putting his car to an inferior and irrational as well as illegal use.

The trouble is that if once you begin running at thirty miles, twenty seems slow. If you accustom yourself to forty, thirty becomes dull. After sixty, fifty is no better than a crawl. It is best never to fall a victim to the speed mania, and if you habituate yourself to running at fifteen or eighteen, then occasional spins of twenty will give you all the exhilaration you can want. The pleasure is entirely relative – a matter of comparison with your own experience; and if you have once in ignorance become tempted to let yourself fall in love with high speeds, the best thing you can do is to break yourself of it as soon as possible. If you confine yourself sternly for a few days to a maximum rate of twelve miles or so, you will find thereafter that a speed of twenty has all the excitement that formerly you got out of forty. I know not a few motorists who know pretty well all that there is to be known of fast running, and have come back to the conviction that there is more enjoyment in keeping within the speed limit than there is in breaking it. The time, I believe, is coming when it will be just as bad form to scorch in a car as it is on a bicycle – when gentlemen and decent folk will no more think of bragging of the speed of their car on the high road than they do today of the speed of their carriage horses.

A Climb up Sna Fell

FROM *COUNTRY LIFE*, 30 MAY 1868 BY HARRY CHILD

Sna Fell (Snow Mountain) is the highest peak on the Isle of Man. Today, the summit can be reached easily – by an electric railway. From it, on a fine day, England, Wales, Scotland and Ireland are all visible. The following, amusing article appeared in *Country Life*, **30 May 1868**

DOUGLAS BAY, in the Isle of Man, is considered one of the prettiest spots in the world. It has often been called the Bay of Naples in miniature. Steaming in from the sea, you observe before you a semicircle of beauty and loveliness. At the outer edges of the bay, right and left, huge fantastic shapen granite rocks rise up out of the sea, the various mosses and shrubs on whose craggy sides tinge them with innumerable colours. Before you is a bold curve of silvery sand, above which, and at some little distance beyond, rise dense clusters of trees; while in the centre may be seen Castle Mona, its long white façade being conspicuous amidst the deep green of the surrounding foliage. Many small villas peep out here and there, and most of the houses being white, at a distance they look like fragments of chalk dotted about, and lying upon a bed of moss. To the left the Fort Sun Hotel, built half-way up the rock, appears with its mimic battlements and towers, like a toy castle or fortress. A break in the circular belt of green occurs where a crowded mass of buildings, with the pier and the lighthouse, mark the site of the town of Douglas. Beyond and towering above all are the mountains, sometimes sharply defined against the bright blue sky, and at others lost in dim and misty vapour. In the centre of the bay stands the Tower of Refuge, a small building erected upon a rocky pinnacle, which at low water juts up just above the surface. The sea here is celebrated for its extreme transparency. Leaning over the bulwarks of the steamer, and looking down into the calm pellucid water, you may easily watch the movements of the fish far below the surface. The delicate tint of the water, the deeper and more varied hues of the craggy rocks, the dark green shade of the foliage of the trees, the distant mountains partially enveloped in a thin purple haze, and the bright blue sky above dotted with fleecy clouds lazily sailing along before the light summer breeze; this piece of charming scenery is worthy of the magic brush of Turner.

In Douglas I met a rambling atom of humanity, like myself. In two days we had exhausted all the sights and novelties of the town and immediate neighbourhood; looked at, wondered at and admired, everything, from the most venerated relic of antiquity down to the far-famed tailless cats of the island. The high peaks of Sna Fell and its sister pinnacles, piercing the clouds, were visible from the streets. After some little consultation, we resolved to visit the summit of the King of the Manx mountains.

It was a bright morning in August when we prepared to start. A young Manx urchin was the only guide we could obtain. For the munificent sum of eighteenpence he agreed to pilot the way to the top. We started off, and soon left the noise of Douglas behind. From the town the summit of the mountain looked surprisingly near, but a walk of two hours scarcely brought us to the foot. About noon we arrived at a farmhouse perched upon one of the mountain spurs. It stood alone, far distant from any other habitation. Before the door were two pretty Manx lassies, with short petticoats and home-made carelessly-constructed bonnets, which if not of a fashionable shape, were exceedingly picturesque. They were ignorant of the approach of strangers until they heard our footsteps upon the stones before the door, when suddenly turning their heads with a startled motion, they made a hasty survey of the intruders, and, with their rosy sunburnt faces growing darker still with blushes, they both rushed indoors and disappeared. The old farmer, aroused and alarmed by the flutter and excitement of his daughters, appeared, and after a little explanation, invited us inside. The roof of the hut was low and the rafters well blackened with smoke. The floor was clay and the walls were built of rubble, and extremely thick. On one side was an immense chimney, immense for the size of the building, with the dying embers of a wood fire on the hearth. An old woman sat near the small square window, spinning wool with the now seldom-seen hand spinning-wheel. The farmer informed us he sheared his own sheep, and with the wool made his own cloth, and showed us a specimen. It would not have suited Mr Poole, but it answered the purpose for which clothes were, as I believe, originally intended – it kept out the weather. We asked for beer and bread and cheese, but could only get buttermilk and oatcake. We had brought some cold milk punch, but reserved it for periods of greater distress. This primitive family, finding we were Londoners, listened with deep interest to our account of the Great City, but the bashfulness and modesty of the two daughters never entirely disappeared, and we now and then caught them making reconnoitering peeps round the doorpost. The weather being fearfully sultry, we proposed leaving our coats at the farm, and continuing the ascent in our shirt-sleeves. Fortunately for us, the farmer persuaded us not to make so foolish an experiment.

We continued our ascent. It was a terrible pull up the steep grassy slope, but the labour was well repaid, as we occasionally looked back and saw the grand panorama below, which gave us some slight inkling of the magnificent view we should obtain from the summit. After innumerable rests and many sips of cold milk punch, from a large flat doctor's bottle, the top was gained. It was a comparatively flat surface, covered with a kind of black spongy, peaty earth, sprinkled over with loose pieces of spar. Although we had felt the heat so oppressive down below, the wind up here blew keen and cutting as in December.

But the view! – it was magnificent in the extreme. Around, as far as the eye could reach, was the sea, calm and tranquil, bathed in the fierce light of the sun; while close down under the mountain we could trace the irregular outline of the coast. Around us rose the other peaks of the Manx mountains – North Barrule, Bein-y-phot, double-headed Garrahan, pyramid-like Greaba, lonely Sliewhallen, South Barrule, and Cronknaireylha. The island appeared like a floating emerald upon the wide waste of waters; and, strange as it may seem, a feeling of insecurity crept over us as we beheld the apparent smallness of the spot of green earth on which we were standing. But the sea – the wide waste of waters stretching out far and wide on every side, was the sight which most engrossed our attention. It appeared calm and smooth as a sheet of glass, save one broad golden path where the reflection of the sun enabled us to perceive the slightly broken water dancing and quivering in his beams.

To the east we saw a patch of vapour hanging far away upon the horizon, and to the north and west we noticed the same dim, scarcely traceable, outlines of what we thought clouds. Our juvenile guide informed us that the apparent low cloud to the east was part of England, that to the north part of Scotland and, that to the west, Ireland. We found a shelter from the wind made by the shepherds of clods of turf. Here we sat for a couple of hours dreamily watching the tiny specks of white sails far away on the horizon, or the long, dark trail

of smoke as it issued from the funnel of a steamer, and curiously hung horizontally over the sea for miles; every part of it being equidistant from the surface. The wind blew terribly keen, and our young guide was shivering like a wet dog, so taking a last look at the fair scene around we proposed to descend.

'You don't want me to go down with you, sir, do you gentlemen,' said the young urchin, 'I want to go over to my uncle's, t'other side o' here, and I shall stop all night?'

This sounded like revolt; and if the unprincipled little fellow had left us we should have found some difficulty in reaching Douglas that night. In the west clouds were already gathering, and it is not unusual for these mountains to be rapidly enveloped in mist and vapour, when even the most experienced shepherds have difficulty in tracing the sheep paths. My friend suddenly snatched the boy's cap from his head by way of hostage, and the article being nearly a new one, this act led to negotiations. After a while he offered to take us down by a different route, much prettier than the one by which we had ascended, if we gave him another 'bob'. Giving him another shilling, we ordered him to proceed. My friend, however, refused to return his cap, arguing with great wisdom and knowledge of human nature, that if the little imp broke through his first bargain what was there to compel him to faithfully fulfil the second. So the Manx lad toddled on bare-headed, which was after all no great hardship, but rather a benefit, for the breeze blew his thick hair about, performing the office of a comb and brush, which articles I firmly believe he never used.

The way was different with a venge-ance. In one part especially the side of the mountain was as steep as an old gable roof. We were obliged to descend sideways, stooping low and putting our hands upon the turf as additional safety.

'If you wuz to begin to roll here, sir, you'd never stop till you got to the bottom, and then you'd be dead,' said our juvenile pilot.

This information naturally increased our care in descending. Presently we heard a shout of distress from our guide. I looked round and found he had disappeared. We both looked down the mountain in horror, expecting to see his unfortunate little carcass bounding down below, a shapeless mass of humanity. We could see nothing, but a prolonged yelling told us he was close at hand, although not in sight. We ultimately found he had fallen into a wide crevice, covered with grass, whence bubbled a little stream, which ran on trickling down the side of the mountain. We pulled him out, and found that the cause of his clamour was not pain but fear. He informed us, with terror stamped on every feature, that the spring was haunted by fairies, and that from the valley below he had often on dark nights seen lights bobbing about the spot.

We continued our descent, and near the foot of the mountain met with an exquisite gem of scenery, worthy of the brush of Constable. It was a romantic leafy nook – a poet's corner of natural loveliness – a little dell of wild beauty. The clear sparkling water of the mountain stream – the same whose birthplace we had seen higher up – came leaping from a half-decayed moss-grown trough, and fell upon an old water-wheel, which lazily obeyed the impulse of the fluid, the creaking of its rough wooden axis

'Cascade at Ambleside' (1786) by Francis Towne (1739-1816); pen and ink and watercolour. (*Ashmolean Museum, Oxford*)

seeming like a groan of complaint at being hurried forward. Sometimes it would dash round quickly and furiously, as though enraged with its state of eternal thraldom; at others it would gradually slacken its speed as though about to stop and question the right of the water to disturb it from rest and indolence. But then the stream would splash and splutter, and bubble, and fling about its spray, and pitilessly pelt the lazy old wheel with its irresistible spirit of motion, until at last the cumbrous machine would again whirl forward, giving a creaking groan of rage and despair. And so they went on, the wheel grumbling at its fate like a worn-out overworked being, wishing to die away into inactivity, the wild, dashing, mountain stream, like a teasing, wilful spirit, constantly goading it into life and motion. Above and around was a leafy screen of limes, elms, oaks and shrubs, through which the glimmering light of the setting sun fell in uncertain and quivering rays, gilding in patches the flowery banks of the stream, and the moss-covered pebbles and stones, and as the spray from the revolving wheel fell across the beams of light these liquid atoms became for the moment tinged with all the colours and soft shades of the rainbow.

At last a man came from out the roughly built hut close by, and shutting off the tormenting stream into another channel, it plunged unimpeded into the watercourse below, and the wheel slowly relapsed into a state of rest and tranquillity, its wooden axis giving a prolonged sigh of relief and content as it did so.

We sat some time, enjoying the solitude, watching the mimic waterfall softly murmuring, admiring the feathery spray, and breathing the pure mountain air, laden with the fragrance of innumerable wild flowers, and thought of the magic words of Scott:

The western waves of ebbing day,
Rolled o'er the glen their level ray,

The British Library, London

which were peculiarly appropriate to the scene before us.

No one can live upon poetry. Much as we felt inclined to watch the crimson rays of the dying sun painting with a mystic finger the green banks and brown weatherstained wheel with golden light – struggling through the foliage, and casting on the opposite side a lacework of sunlight and shade – flinging strange shadows into the water, and for the moment making every dancing atom of spray globules of the most enchanting and delicate prismatic colours. Much as we admired the soft tints and beauty of the scene, there were grumblings in the viscera which at last forced the mind to dwell upon ham and eggs, and cakes and tea. Four ounces of oatcake, a pint of buttermilk, and about half a pint of milk punch was all we had had since the morning. I believe this, in quantity, is below prison fare. Mind, I am not speaking from experience.

Two miles further on, we entered a village consisting of about six houses, built up irrespective of unity or streets. All of them whitewashed, and one labelled in large black letters Hacon Hotel. We entered the hotel, and found, as Dr Johnson says of his Highland hostelrie, the negative catalogue of provisions was very plentiful. It had a clay floor, smoke-dried rafters, and a fire on the hearth. Five fine, rosy-cheeked children were seated around a deal table in the centre. The landlady, just as we entered, was in the act of turning the contents of a large kettle or pot into a dish on the table – the contents being potatoes and fresh herrings, boiled together. It was exceedingly comical to see the heads and tails of the fish sticking out of the steaming mass of potatoes at all angles, and in every direction. The other inhabitants of the 'hotel' consisted of several cocks and hens, strutting about with all the majesty and dignity usually assumed by those self-sufficient and conceited bipeds; one proud pompous fellow occasionally crowing most lustily, and perching himself on the backs of the chairs, on the rafters, and on the opened door with the most amusing impudence. There was likewise an extremely persevering, energetic pig – joint proprietor or guest of the 'hotel'. It was droll to see him squatting on his hams, and sitting upright like a dog, keenly watching for pieces of potato as they dropped from the table. When any fell, he gave a grunt of satisfaction, and delight, and rushed pell-mell after it, irrespective of table-legs, chairs, or stools; and often in his anxiety to reach the dainty morsel, the stool on which the youngest child sat (whose weight was not sufficient to fix it so tightly to the ground as the others) was obliged to be rescued from falling by the ever-ready hand of the mother, who each time threatened the offending pig with eternal banishment, but never seemed inclined to carry out the threat, believing, no doubt, that a good fat ham in the winter, would be much better than an empty dish. Master Piggy did not have it all his own way. There were other claimants in the field. The feathered community did not recognise his title to the waifs and strays. They disputed his claim as lord of the manor, and many tough fights ensued. It was amusing to watch the different military tactics of the combatants. The squadron of poultry fought as skirmishers; they carried on a desultory warfare as guerillas, charging and retreating with the rapidity of a light brigade; while the pig, tightly shutting his eyes and trusting to the thickness and semi-impenetrability of his hide, would plunge and lumber in amongst them, producing the same effect as a ponderous iron-clad would amongst a number of little cockle-shell boats.

As the larder of the 'hotel' afforded nothing better, we partook of the supper. Hungry as we were, we dived into the steaming pyramid of potatoes and fished out the defunct herrings with a heartiness and avidity worthy of a better dish. Beer we also had. It was small beer – and I must add very small beer indeed; the alcohol in it bearing about the same proportion to the liquid, as one drop of spirit would to the volume of water in all the seas in the world. It was like cold toast and water, made bitter. For the meal we were charged twopence per head, and the retail price of the beer was one penny per quart. Surely the proprietor could successfully resist the imputation of exorbitant charges.

Long shall I remember the 'hotel' in the hills – long shall I remember the large, low, square, smoke-dried room which served as dining-room, sitting-room and bedroom, pantry, kitchen, and scullery; pigsty, and hen-house, cellar, bar, and bar-parlour. It was dark when we left, and the sun had long before rolled down the western sky a ball of golden fire, sinking into the sea amidst a gorgeous mass of purple and crimson clouds.

As we were walking home, our guide amused us with an account of the *Mauthe Dhoogh*, the great spectre-hound which once haunted Peel Castle. It must have possessed a most insatiable appetite, and extraordinary power of digestion, gobbling up, according to tradition, between sunset and sunrise every human being that crossed its path. It seems the *Mauthe Dhoogh* had a weakness for the military, enjoying the mastication of a soldier with the same gastronomic delight as an alderman does the disposal of a piece of green turtle-fat. He also related several wild legends connected with the mountain fairies. 'Did you ever see any of them?' I asked. 'No, sir, but my grandfather knew somebody who did.' That's the worst of these fairies – they never appear to anyone except a man's grandfather's fourth cousin's wife's friend's friend, or some other person equally remote, who can never be found. We must believe in them, however, for the sake of Titania, Oberon, Puck, Ariel, and several other old familiar friends of the same fraternity.

As we approached Douglas, we looked back. The moon had risen, and its pale beams cast a flood of soft, silvery light on the gaunt outline of Sna Fell.

We reluctantly turned our faces towards the comparatively dim, murky gaslight of the town, and left the mountains to the elves and moonlight.

Meadow Grasses

BY HENRY WILLIAMSON (1895-1977)

Henry Williamson was known for his sensitive and unsentimental approach to nature. His novel Tarka the Otter **(1927) was one of the books which established his reputation. The following piece, written in 1920, is from** The Lone Swallows and Other Essays of Boyhood and Youth **(1933)**

A BRIMSTONE butterfly drifted with the wind over the waving grasses, and settled on the shallow cup of a tall flower, John-go-to-bed-at-noon. The bright flowers were closing, for the sun was high. It paused for an instant only, and then fluttered over the hedge and was gone. Came a common white butterfly – a weed of the air, hated by the countrymen: yet part of summer's heart as it flickered like a strayed snowflake in the sunshine, passing the whorled spires of red-green sorrel and glazed petals of buttercup, living its brief hour among the scents and colours of summer.

Vibrating their sun-crisped wings with shrill hum, the hover-flies shot past: the wild humble-bees sang to themselves as in a frenzy of labour for their ideal they took the pollen from the roses in the hedge; the cuckoos sent call after call of melody from the distant hazel coppice. The sound of summer was everywhere, the earth filled with swelling ecstasy – everything so green and alive, the waving grasses and the hawthorns; the green kingdom charged and surcharged with energy, from the wild strawberry to the mighty, sap-surfeited bole of the oak. Although so still, the vast earth was humming and vibrating, the crescendo of passion reached gradually while the sun swept nearer, day by day, the zenith of its curve.

In one corner of the meadow was a small pond, half hidden by rushes, bearing a golden blazon of flower – in autumn the country people would grind the roasted seeds of the iris to make their 'poor man's coffee'. With them grew the bog asphodel, crowned by a tapering spike of starlike flowers, also yellow, the colour of happiness: in old time this plant was supposed to soften the bones of cattle, hence the Latin name, *ossifragum*. Hidden securely among the rushes, the moorhen had her nest of dried water-weed, a platform on which at night rested her children, little black balls of fluff with red beeks. A faint chirruping came from the flags, a splash, and silence: the mother had heard my slow approach and called to her young to remain still.

Something with a thin, stick-like body, enamelled blue and fanned by a whirling crystal of light, alighted on the open white petals of a crowsfoot – the water-buttercup; the dragonfly folded its gauzy wings and contemplated the still deeps from which, a few hours before, it had crept – a summer thing that would fulfil its destiny so quickly, and die. Like the civilised bees that leave the security of skep and stored caves of honey to the new race, so all the wild things live but to secure the future of their species. Everything strives for the beautiful, the ideal, without conscious effort, maybe, but the ideal is there – all for the species. The nightingale that silvers the dusk with song has finer notes than his ancestor of olden time; he has learnt so much during the centuries; through generations of faithful loyalty to an ideal his tiny soul-flame has become brighter, and his voice speaks with sweeter poetry. On the may trees in the hedge, already shaking their blossoms into the wind, the wild roses were open to the sky; it was now their brief hour of sunshine. Simple petals stained with roseal hue, they waited for the wild bee to bring the pollen that would change the beauty into life.

High sang the larks over the meadow, striving with fluttering wings to reach the blue vision of heaven. Their voices trailed to the earth and filled the heart with hope and joy. Afar, the noisy rooks fed their young in the colony in the elm tops; at hand, on the ground, golden buttercup and white moon-daisy, lemon-coloured hawk-weed and obstinate charlock, beloved of the visiting bee for its great dowry of honey. The sunbeams had flooded the cold earth during the springtide of the year, and now the earth had sent its flowers and its grasses with their faces turned above, whence came the light that was life, the light that was truth to the birds and the bees, the flowers and the grasses. Men ponder the higher meaning of life, studying in cities, amid the smoke and clattering hum of traffic; the wild ones have never needed to seek – they have been happy by the brook with its lanced sunpoints and swallowy song of summer over the pebbles and the mossy boulders; they have had no illusions. They have not needed philosophies or discarnate paradises.

Everything loved the mowing meadow. By the stream the blackbirds sought for food, the finches came to sip, the hover-flies fanned above the kingcups. Scarlet soldier flies and little plain moths clung to bennet-bloom and spray-like awn, the wind sighed in the grasses as it shook the dust-pollen from the heads. The meadow grasses were timorous of the breeze, and trembled at its coming, like the heart of a maiden reluctant yet yearning: whispering to the wind to bear the seeds, for the mowers would come shortly. Over the water-meadow the lapwings wheeled and spun – the lapwing holds the secret of the swamps and boglands, and you hear it in his wild voice as his wings sough above. In the early spring he makes over the dull furrows his plaintive music, climbing high and diving to the ground as though it were sweet ecstasy to fall, wing-crumpled and broken-hearted, before his mate. Something in the call of the peewit fills me with sadness, like the memory of those passed springs that were in boyhood so glamorous. The peewit's song is wild, he knows that all things pass, that the leaves and the flowers will die and nothing remain.

Now, as he saw me, his voice was harsher, more husky; somewhere among the tufts of spiked grass his young were crouching, depending on their plumage in harmony with the ground to remain unseen. *See-oo-sweet, see-oo-sweet, woo*, cried the mother: her curled crest was visible against the sky as she turned on broad pinions.

One morning, when the cuckoo was silent and the young partridges were following their parents through the culms of the meadow-forest, two labourers arrived with the mowing machine, drawn by a pair of chestnut horses. The overture to the midsummer hum was beginning to be heard in the fields: wild and tame bees ceased not from their labours; the wolf spiders were everywhere in the long grass, searching for fly or insect in their blood lust. Another kind of spider had erected a net-like web between the stalks, with a round silky tunnel in the middle, in which he crouched among the skins of beetles, glowing a dull bronzy green in the sun; the torn wings of a red admiral butterfly never again to pass with colour-dusty sails above the blue scabious flowers; all the tragic remainder of his catch scattered like jetsam at the sea's marge. The larks still sang into the sunshine. It was the time of year, just past the fullness of young summer, when the song of visitant birds was over and the insect hum had begun its shimmering undertone.

The mowing machine, drawn by the glossy-coated horses, moved down one side of the field. One of the mowers sat on the iron seat and drove the pair; his mate walked alongside and scooped the cut grasses from the knives with a rake. The horses tossed their manes and swished their tails, drawing along with magnificent power the light machine, and leaving behind a swathe of broken grasses and coloured flowers whose fragrance and hue availed no longer – in an instant the life was gone – whither?

Rhythmically they moved in straight line, the clattering of the machine mingling with the cries of the driver: like a sea-green wave overcurled and spent in foam the flowery grasses lay in the sun. Cat's-tail grass, foxtail grass, meadow soft grass, pale red in tint and sometimes called Yorkshire fog; couch grass – the *agropyron* of ancient Greece – the wild kin of the wheat; the sweet-smelling vernal grass without whose presence one of the fleeting

83

scents of summer were denied us. Steadily the mowing machine was drawn round the field, fresh wallow lay where but a moment before the meadow-forest bowed and returned to the wind, and the dandelion wrought its goldened disk in the image of the sun. With the lilac flower of the scabious lay the incarnadine head of the poppy – tokening sleep that now had claimed its own. Meadow-crane's bill, which had overtopped the grasses with the wine-dark sorrel and prickly thistle, the vetch, and the blue speedwell – from the highest to the lowest – all brought low by the skirring knives.

Years ago in an old village the mowers went down into the meadow with their curved scythes, and throughout the long summer day they swung their ancient implements. Every now and then they paused to whet the sap-blurred blades with a stone carried in their belts. *Tu-whet, tu-whaat* – holding the symbol of olden times near the point: it was the extreme edge of the curve that required such constant sharpening. Their hats were bleached by the showers and the sunshine – I do not recollect seeing a new one, but it may have been a faulty impression of childhood. It was thirsty work wielding the scythe on its long handle; wooden 'bottles', or firkins, of ale were brought out in the early morning and hidden in the nettle ditch, well down in the cool and shade; and often a gallon of small ale was drunken by each labourer before the goatsbeard closed its flowers at noon.

The sun bronzed their arms and dried the swathes; colour soon faded. The scarlet poppy shrivelled to a purple brown, the gold of the dandelion became dulled, the grasses wilted as they fell. It was great fun to follow the workers, to gather whole armfuls of flowers, and to pull their petals apart. They were but flowers to me then, pretty things, their colours delighting the eye, so many of them: the boy was natural and thought little, knowing nothing of what the irritable and thwarted seekers in cities of Europe were preparing, unconsciously and half-consciously, for his generation. Very soon swathes of dead youths were lying in ruined cornfields, and the righteous were condemning others for the results of their own unclear ways and thoughts.

In the evening the village girls came into the field to turn the hay when the grass was fully dried by the sun, and nothing remained of luscious clover or disk of corn feverfew. The young larks or corncrakes, caught perchance by the rasping sweep of scythes, had been dead many days. They raked the harvest of the meadow into mound-like wakes, while the master haymaker, ever watching the clouds and the wind, urged them to greater endeavour, for rain meant a second-rate crop; and continued rain, complete loss.

We tossed wisps of hay at one another, and formed ourselves into rival parties, each with its castle, and defied our enemies with shrill cries. The lumbering wain came back from the stack, a host of flies pestering the horse, who stamped and kicked in vain when a gadfly fastened to his side and drew

'The Haymakers' (1785) by George Stubbs (1724-1806); oils. (*The Tate Gallery, London*)

his blood. If the weather were fine, and no danger of rain impending, the carter would, as a great treat, let us ride on the broad back of the horse, who appreciated the fan of wych-elm twigs that was whisked about his ears and eyes.

No other meadows can be the same, the flowers there were fairer, the sunlight brighter as it followed the clouds. With so many summers burnt out in autumnal fires there is a dearer thought for every flower of blue chicory: and each germander speedwell, so common in the hedgerow, has in its little petals something of the mystery of the sky. The breath of all the springtimes, the light and shade of summery months, the colour and song of the fields stored, layer upon layer, in the boy's mind, return a hundredfold, and with them a desire, never ceasing, for others to share in this secret of happiness – the thoughts given by nature.

They were happy days – gone now with the wielders of the scythes in their faded hats and their wooden ale-bottles. Now the knives of the mowing machine shear the field in half a day; the happy girls no longer turn the swathes in the evening. The old spirit of the country is dying, for the spirit of the factory and the town has overlaid it. The 'big house' is sold, and a new squire has arrived, a merchant and a rich man; the sons of the old squire lie somewhere in the deep sea near Jutland, so why retain the estate, heavily taxed and scarce self-supporting, when it will eventually pass away into other hands?

I have come to know other meadows now, but they can never be quite the same. I lie in the flowery fields, seeing the quaking grass against the sky, and a wild bee swinging on a blue columbine, while a lark rains joy from on high. These return, these are eternal; and with them a voice that is silent, a glance that is gone.

'To and fro our keen scythes go; down sinks the purple clover'. From *The Quiver*, November, 1870.
(*The British Library, London*)

Cavalcade of
Summer Riches

BY J. H. B. PEEL

J. H. B. Peel, who is firstly a poet, lives in North Devon but loves, and comments on, rural life all over the British Isles. He also writes the fortnightly Saturday essay 'Country Talk' in *The Daily Telegraph***, where 'Cavalcade of Summer Riches' first appeared. It is also to be found in** *Country Talk Continued* **(Hale)**

THE word 'summer' comes from the Sanskrit *asma*, meaning 'half-year'. Like the year itself, summer is divided into seasons, low summer, midsummer, high summer.

Low summer is scarcely more advanced than high spring because several species of migrant birds have only lately arrived, and the woods shine as they did in May. Midsummer is more spacious. From dawn till dusk the sun spans our waking hours and overlaps them with a long arc which George Meredith drew with a short line:

This was a day that knew not age.

High summer bestows almost a surfeit of colour and scent, for the corn is yellowing, the chrysanthemums are flowering and the honeysuckle yields a second crop. Dismiss the climate as a joke, or curse it as a catastrophe, still you must admit that an English summer day can be among the loveliest on Earth and better suited than any other to our temperate needs. Between May and August a countryman usually awakes to Ronsard's welcome: '*La vierge, la vivace, et le bel aujourd'hui.*'

Some people are so enamoured of summer that their urge to prolong it causes a mild amnesia which persists until the evidence compels them to confess: 'It must be nearly a month since the longest day.' Much will depend on the weather. If June and July were dismal we bid them good riddance and pin our hopes on August and September; but if June and July fulfilled their promise we remain true to them, and would, if we could, live with them for ever.

Returning home after a week's absence in high summer, you find that the sun and the rain have transformed the garden. A tardy petunia's single bloom has multiplied itself four-fold. The antirrhinums are in full flower, even in the cold north-eastern counties. A handful of rosebuds

'Gathering Plums' by Henry H. La Thangue (1859-1929); oils. (*City of Manchester Art Galleries*)

have become a bedful of roses. Wayside cow-parsley or Queen Anne's lace, whose flowers were no larger than a florin when you left, are now the size of a saucer.

Every season contains the seeds of its successor and the ashes of its predecessor. Toward the middle of July, for instance, the birds by their noonday silence announce that summer has reached its meridian. The deciduous trees wear a dark uniform; only the holly enjoys a belated spring, glossy while the rest have lost their sheen. Grass reaches its maximum height. Sheep are shorn. Skeins of blackberries thrust tentacles across the lane, as though to welcome early autumn. Everything looks luxuriantly lush.

Watching the cavalcade with unemotive precision, science is careful to exclude imagination from its analysis. James Thomson, on the other hand,

blended fact with fantasy when he viewed the ripening wheat and the plumping fruit. 'There is,' he declared, 'no thinking of these things without breaking into poetry.' So, into poetry he broke:

'Tis raging noon; and, vertical, the sun
Darts on the head direct his forceful
    rays.
O'er heaven and earth, far as the
    ranging eye
Can sweep, a dazzling deluge reigns . . .

Thomson allowed, however, that the English summer may unleash a very different sort of deluge:

Down comes a deluge of sonorous hail,
Or prone-descending rain. Wind-rent,
    the clouds
Pour a whole flood . . .

Wet or dry, decay is a condition of rebirth, at any rate among many plants. Invisible among undergrowth, the shrivelled bluebells are even now preparing their annual resurrection. The daffodils are neither dead nor sleeping. Next year's leaf is already an indenture on the twig.

Despite the corn harvest and a second crop of hay, the farmer's wife finds time to cultivate her old favourites in a garden where Dorothy Perkins rambles pinkly round the door; where honeysuckle hides the wall of a derelict privy; where sweet williams cluster alongside asters and dahlias; where forget-me-nots weave a summer sky for pansies, marigolds, foxgloves.

This cavalcade is no less vivid in meadows dappled with sorrel, campion, poppy, charlock, hemlock, herb robert, wild carrot, scabious, teasel, sheep's vetch, and the perennial daisy. There, too, the last of the lambs still run with the ewes and hedgerows proffer a posy of roses.

Most townsfolk regard July as a holiday season; but people in deep country, where agriculture is still the chief occupation, regard July as a crescendo of hard labour and anxious anticipation. In parts of Scotland the crofters are still haymaking and throughout Britain the arable farmers already know whether the grain crop has the makings of a heavy one. What they do not know, and seem unlikely ever to discover, is whether a drought or a downpour will dash their great expectations. Such men feel little  interest in Walt Whitman's holiday hankering:

> O to sail a ship!
> To leave the tiresome sameness of the
> streets . . .

A cottager glances at the logs in his woodshed and then forgets them because the sun provides both light and warmth. Next month, no doubt, he will quiz those logs more closely, saying: 'The evenings are drawing in. We'll soon need a fire.' Meanwhile, sufficient unto the season are the boons thereof, pressed down and overflowing.

A Visit to a Farm

BY RICHARD GRAVES (1715-1804)

Richard Graves was a country parson with literary leanings. The following is an extract from his two charming little volumes entitled *Eugenius or Anecdotes of the Golden Vale* **(1785). The author introduces Eugenius as 'an old schoolfellow from one of the midland counties' who 'has a passion for the wild beauties of nature'. One summer, Eugenius's friend Williams of Jesus College, Oxford, invited him to his father's house 'situated in a sequestered vale, in the most mountainous part of North Wales'. Llan-dryffyd dur Llwiffen 'which the gentlemen recently settled there not being able to pronounce' has come to be known as 'The Golden Vale'. A few years later, Eugenius makes a return visit to see his friends there . . .**

ONE afternoon young Williams, Miss Flora and myself took a walk of three miles to visit their elder sister who had married a wealthy farmer, a Mr Owen, with about an hundred pounds a year free land.

When we came near the house, Miss Flora would have run before, to apprise her sister of our approach; as she said we should certainly find her in a dishabille. To this, however, I would by no means consent, as I wished to see my old acquaintance transformed into a farmer's wife.

When we came to the gate, I looked over, and saw what was to me a very pleasing *picture*, in the style of Berhem.

The maid was milking the cows under the shade of an old elm, where the patient animals were assembled, gently ruminating, and waiting their turns to be eased of their salubrious burden – a little boy and girl were feeding the poultry; and in a chair at the door Mrs Owen was sitting, with a Madonna air, hanging over and suckling her child.

If the ladies were thoroughly sensible to the beauty of that attitude – and the infinite advantages, both to themselves and to their children, of that *indispensable* duty – one would think it impossible for them to resign that pleasure to a mercenary woman; who may (and I fear often does) communicate disease and bad temper to the most healthy infants.

Though Mrs Owen retained nothing more of her boarding-school education than the gold wires in her ears – yet, thus properly employed, she appeared to me superior to a lady of the first rank,

92

'The Outhouse' by William Henry Hunt (1790-1864); watercolour.
(*Reproduced by permission of the Syndics of the Fitzwilliam Museum, Cambridge*)

Engraving by Myles Birket Foster (1825-99) which appeared in the book *English Country Life* (1859) by Thomas Miller. (*The British Library, London*)

dressed out at a rout or a card-table.

Mrs Owen started up at the sight of us, covering her bosom, and gathering up her hair, which hung in ringlets over her neck; and ran in to adjust her dress.

Flora Williams began to make apologies for her sister, as she said she had three children to take care of, and a dairy to inspect, and manage a large family, and the like.

My dear Miss Williams, said I, don't you yet know me better? That I am a zealous and constant votary of nature, and an enthusiastic admirer of all her operations and productions? How beautiful is each motion and attitude of these animals! – the hen, anxious to point out the grain to her infant progeny – the playful gambols of those heifers, and their unaffected surprise at the approach of strangers. I had rather see you, Flora, lovely as you are now, in the same situation with your sister, than dressed for the play or the Lady Mayoress's ball. She was employed virtuously and with *propriety*, which is always pleasing. If I were to fall in love with a cook-maid, it would be when she was beating up the fire with her poker, or winding up the jack; and not when she was stuck out on a Sunday with her fan and scoured silk gown, and studying airs at the parlour looking-glass.

Mrs Owen now appeared, and gave us some tea, and a quart bowl of cream strewd with brown sugar. But the most delicious treat I enjoyed while young Williams walked out to look after his brother-in-law, and Mrs Owen was busy with her family, was half a quarter of an

The Farm Yard, an illustration from Tom Taylor's *Pictures of an English Landscape* (1862) by Myles Birket Foster (1825-99). (*The British Library, London*)

hour's tête-à-tête with Flora Williams. After fixing a day for Mrs Owen to bring her children to her father's, we took our leave, and had a delightful walk home. In the company of a friend, and of so amiable a female companion, the mere clouds, gilded by the setting sun – the purple tint in the mountains – the stillness of the evening, sweetly enlivened by the thrilling notes of the nightingale – all conspired to produce that tranquillity of soul, which is the height of human felicity.

'Ancient Farmer's Wife', an anonymous engraving. (*The British Museum, London*)

A Tour in Scotland

BY DOROTHY WORDSWORTH (1771-1855)

William Wordsworth's devoted sister, Dorothy, was the chronicler of events around their home neighbourhood of Grasmere, and also of a Scottish tour she made with her brother accompanied by their great friend Samuel Taylor Coleridge. The following extract is from her diary of this visit to Scotland

WE found the ferryman at work in the field above his hut, and he was at liberty to go with us, but, being wet and hungry, we begged that he would let us sit by his fire till we had refreshed ourselves. This was the first genuine Highland hut we had been in. We entered by the cow-house, the house door being within, at right angles to the outer door. The woman was distressed that she had a bad fire, but she heaped up some dry peats and heather, and, blowing it with her breath, in a short time raised a blaze that scorched us into comfortable feelings. A small part of the smoke found its way out of the hole of the chimney, the rest through the open window-places, one of which was within the recess of the fireplace, and made a frame to a little picture of the restless lake and the opposite shore, seen when the outer door was open. The woman of the house was very kind: whenever we asked her for anything it seemed a fresh pleasure to her that she had it for us; she always answered with a sort of softening down of the Scotch exclamation,

Loch Achray by Myles Birket Foster.
(*The British Library, London*)

'Hoot!' 'Ho! yes, ye'll get that,' and hied to her cupboard in the spence. We were amused with the phrase 'Ye'll get that' in the Highlands, which appeared to us as if it came from a perpetual feeling of the difficulty with which most things are procured. We got oatmeal, butter,

97

bread and milk, made some porridge, and then departed. It was rainy and cold, with a strong wind.

Coleridge was afraid of the cold in the boat, so he determined to walk down the lake, pursuing the same road we had come along. There was nothing very interesting for the first three or four miles on either side of the water: to the right, uncultivated heath or poor coppice-wood, and to the left, a scattering of meadow ground, patches of corn, copp-ice-woods, and here and there a cottage. The wind fell, and it began to rain heavily. On this William wrapped himself in the boatman's plaid, and lay at the bottom of the boat till we came to a place where I could not help rousing him.

We were rowing down that side of the lake which had hitherto been little else than a moorish ridge. After turning a rocky point we came to a bay closed in by rocks and steep woods, chiefly of full-grown birch. The lake was elsewhere ruffled, but at the entrance of this bay the breezes sunk, and it was calm: a small island was near, and the opposite shore, covered with wood, looked soft through the misty rain. William, rubbing his eyes, for he had been asleep, called out that he hoped I had not let him pass by anything that was so beautiful as this; and I was glad to tell him that it was but the beginning of a new land. After we had left this bay we saw before us a long reach of woods and rocks and rocky points, that promised other bays more beautiful than what we had passed. The ferryman was a good-natured fellow, and rowed very industriously, following the ins and outs of the shore; he was delighted with the pleasure we expressed, continually repeating how pleasant it would have been on a fine day. I believe he was attached to the lake by some sentiment of pride, as his own domain – his being almost the only boat upon it – which made him, seeing we were willing gazers, take far more pains than an ordinary boatman; he would often say, after he had compassed the turning of a point, 'This is a bonny part,' and he always chose the bonniest, with greater skill than our prospect-hunters and 'picturesque travellers'; places screened from the winds – that was the first point; the rest followed of course – richer growing trees, rocks and banks, and curves which the eye delights in.

The second bay we came to differed from the rest; the hills retired a short space from the lake, leaving a few level fields between, on which was a cottage embosomed in trees: the bay was de-fended by rocks at each end, and the hills behind made a shelter for the cottage, the only dwelling, I believe, except one, on this side of Loch Ketterine. We now came to steeps that rose directly from the lake, and passed by a place called in the Gaelic the Den of the Ghosts [Goblins' Cave] which reminded us of Lodore; it is a rock, or mass of rock, with a stream of large black stones like the naked or dried-up bed of a torrent down the side of it; birch-trees start out of the rock in every direction, and cover the hill above, further than we could see. The water of the lake below was very deep, black, and calm. Our delight in-creased as we advanced, till we came in view of the termination of the lake, seeing where the river issues out of it through a narrow chasm between the hills.

Here I ought to rest, as we rested, and attempt to give utterance to our pleasure: but indeed I can impart but little of what we felt. We were still on the same side of

A crofter's house at Loch Ewe, Wester Ross (1889). (*Radio Times Hulton Picture Library*)

the water, and, being immediately under the hill, within a considerable bending of the shore, we were enclosed by hills all round, as if we had been upon a smaller lake of which the whole was visible. It was an entire solitude; and all that we beheld was the perfection of loveliness and beauty.

We had been through many solitary places since we came into Scotland, but this place differed as much from any we had seen before, as if there had been nothing in common between them; no thought of dreariness or desolation found entrance here; yet nothing was to be seen but water, wood, rocks, and heather, and bare mountains above. We saw the mountains by glimpses as the clouds passed by them, and were not disposed to regret, with our boatman, that it was not a fine day, for the near objects were not concealed from us, but softened by being seen through the mists. The lake is not very wide here, but appeared to be much narrower than it really is, owing to the many promontories, which are pushed so far into it that they are much more like islands than promontories. We had a longing desire to row to the outlet and look up into the narrow passage through which the river went; but the point where we were to land was on the other side, so we bent our course right across, and just as we came in sight of two huts, which have been built by Lady Perth as a shelter for those who visit the Trossachs, Coleridge hailed us with a shout of triumph from the door of one of them, exulting in the glory of Scotland. The huts stand at a small distance from each

'Loch Lomond' by Anthony Vandyke Copley Fielding (1787-1855); watercolour.
(*City of Manchester Art Galleries*)

other, on a high and perpendicular rock that rises from the bed of the lake. A road, which has a very wild appearance, has been cut through the rock; yet even here, among these bold precipices, the feeling of excessive beautifulness overcomes every other. While we were upon the lake, on every side of us were bays within bays, often more like tiny lakes or pools than bays, and these not in long succession only, but all round, some almost on the broad breast of the water, the promontories shot out so far.

After we had landed we walked along the road to the uppermost of the huts, where Coleridge was standing. From the door of this hut we saw Benvenue opposite to us – a high mountain, but clouds concealed its top; its side, rising directly from the lake, is covered with birch-trees to a great height, and seamed with innumerable channels of torrents; but now there was no water in them, nothing to break in upon the stillness and repose of the scene; nor do I recollect hearing the sound of water from any side, the wind being fallen and the lake perfectly still; the place was all eye, and completely satisfied the sense and the heart. Above and below us, to the right and to the left, were rocks, knolls, and hills, which, wherever anything could grow – and that was everywhere between the rocks – were covered with trees and heather; the trees did not in any place grow so thick as an ordinary wood; yet I think there was never a bare space of twenty yards: it was more like a natural forest where the trees grow in groups or singly, not hiding the surface of the ground, which, instead of being green and mossy, was of the richest purple. The heather was indeed the most luxuriant I ever saw; it was so tall that a child of ten years old strugg-

Ben Lomond by Myles Birket Foster. (*The British Library, London*)

ling through it would often have been buried head and shoulders, and the exquisite beauty of the colour, near or at a distance, seen under the trees, is not to be conceived. But if I were to go on describing for evermore, I should give but a faint, and very often a false, idea of the different objects and the various combinations of them in this most intricate and delicious place; besides, I tired myself out with describing at Loch Lomond, so I will hasten to the end of my tale. This reminds me of a sentence in a little pamphlet written by the minister of Callander, descriptive of the environs of that place. After having taken up at least six closely-printed pages with the Trossachs, he concludes thus, 'In a word, the Trossachs beggar all description,' – a conclusion in which everybody who has been there will agree with him. I believe the word Trossachs signifies 'many hills': it is a name given to all the eminences at the foot of Loch Ketterine, and about half a mile beyond.

We left the hut, retracing the few yards of road which we had climbed; our boat lay at anchor under the rock in the last of all the compartments of the lake, a small oblong pool, almost shut up within itself, as several others had appeared to be, by jutting points of rock; the termination of a long out-shooting of the water, pushed up between the steps of the main shore where the huts stand, and a broad promontory which, with its hillocks and points and lesser promontories, occupies the centre of the foot of the lake. A person sailing through the lake up the middle of it, would just as naturally suppose that the outlet was here as on the other side; and so it might have been, with the most trifling change in the disposition of the ground, for at the end of this slip of water the lake is confined only by a gentle rising of a few yards towards an opening between the hills, a narrow pass or valley through which the river might have flowed. The road is carried through this valley, which only differs from the lower part of the vale of the lake in being excessively narrow, and without water; it is enclosed by mountains, rocky mounds, hills and hillocks scattered over with birch-trees, and covered with Dutch myrtle and heather, even surpassing what we had seen before. Our mother Eve had no fairer, though a more diversified, garden to tend, than we found within this little close valley. It rained all the time, but the mists and calm air made us ample amends for a wetting.

At the opening of the pass we climbed up a low eminence, and had an unexpected prospect suddenly before us – another lake, small compared with Loch Ketterine, though perhaps four miles long, but the misty air concealed the end of it. The transition from the solitary wildness of Loch Ketterine and the narrow valley or pass to this scene was very delightful: it was a gentle place, with lovely open bays, one small island, cornfields, woods, and a group of cottages. This vale seemed to have been made to be tributary to the comforts of man, Loch Ketterine for the lonely delight of Nature, and kind spirits delighting in beauty. The sky was grey and heavy – floating mists on the hillsides, which softened the objects, and where we lost sight of the lake it appeared so near to the sky that they almost touched one another, giving a visionary beauty to the prospect. While we overlooked this quiet scene we could hear the stream rumbling among the

Loch Katrine by Myles Birket Foster.
(*The British Library, London*)

rocks between the lakes, but the mists concealed any glimpse of it which we might have had. This small lake is called Loch Achray.

We returned, of course, by the same road. Our guide repeated over and over again his lamentations that the day was so bad, though we had often told him – not indeed with much hope that he would believe us – that we were glad of it. As we walked along he pulled a leafy twig from a birch-tree, and, after smelling it, gave it to me, saying, how 'sweet and halesome' it was, and that it was pleasant and very halesome on a fine summer's morning to sail under the banks where the birks are growing. This reminded me of the old Scotch songs, in which you continually hear of the 'pu'ing the birks'. Common as birches are in the north of England, I believe their sweet smell is a thing unnoticed among the peasants. We returned again to the huts to take a farewell look. We had shared our food with the ferryman and a traveller whom we had met here, who was going up the lake, and wished to lodge at the ferry-house,

Ben A'an by Myles Birket Foster. (*The British Library, London*)

so we offered him a place in the boat. Coleridge chose to walk. We took the same side of the lake as before, and had much delight in visiting the bays over again; but the evening began to darken, and it rained so heavily before we had gone two miles that we were completely wet. It was dark when we landed, and on entering the house I was sick with cold.

The good woman had provided, according to her promise, a better fire than we had found in the morning; and indeed when I sate down in the chimney-corner of her smoky biggin' I thought I had never been more comfortable in my life. Coleridge had been there long enough to have a pan of coffee boiling for us, and having put our clothes in the way of drying, we all sate down, thankful for a shelter. We could not prevail upon the man of the house to draw near the fire, though he was cold and wet, or to suffer his wife to get him dry clothes till she had served us, which she did, though most willingly, not very expeditiously. A Cumberland man of the same rank would not have had such a notion of what was fit and right in his own house, or if he had, one would have accused him of servility; but in the Highlander it only seemed like politeness, however erroneous and painful to us, naturally growing out of the dependence of the inferiors of the clan upon their laird; he did not, however, refuse to let his wife bring out the whisky-bottle at our request: 'She keeps a dram,' as the phrase is; indeed, I believe there is scarcely a lonely house by the wayside in Scotland where travellers may not be accommodated with a dram. We asked for sugar, butter, barley-bread, and milk, and with a smile and a stare more of kindness than wonder, she replied, 'Ye'll get that,' bringing each article separately.

We caroused our cups of coffee, laughing like children at the strange atmosphere in which we were: the smoke came in gusts, and spread along the walls and above our heads in the chimney, where the hens were roosting like light clouds in the sky. We laughed and laughed again, in spite of the smarting of our eyes, yet had a quieter pleasure in observing the beauty of the beams and rafters gleaming between the clouds of smoke. They had been crusted over and varnished by many winters, till, where the firelight fell upon them, they were as glossy as black rocks on a sunny day cased in ice. When we had eaten our supper we sate about half an hour, and I think I had one end of the house to the other.

I went to bed some time before the family. The door was shut between us, and they had a bright fire, which I could not see; but the light it sent up among the varnished rafters and beams, which crossed each other in almost as intricate and fantastic a manner as I have seen the under-boughs of a large beech-tree withered by the depth of the shade above, produced the most beautiful effect that can be conceived. It was like what I should suppose an underground cave or temple to be, with a dripping or moist roof, and the moonlight entering in upon it by some means or other, and yet the colours were more like melted gems. I lay looking up till the light of the fire faded away, and the man and his wife and child had crept into their bed at the other end of the room. I did not sleep much, but passed a comfortable night, for my bed, though hard, was warm and clean: the unusualness of my situation prevented me from sleeping. I could hear the waves beat against the shore of the lake; a little 'syke' close to the door made a much louder noise; and when I sate up in my bed I could see the lake through an open window-place at the bed's head. Add to this, it rained all night. I was less occupied by remembrance of the Trossachs, beautiful as they were, than the vision of the Highland hut, which I could not get out of my head. I thought of the Fairyland of Spenser, and what I had read in romance at other times, and then, what a feast would it be for a London pantomime-maker, could he but transplant it to Drury Lane, with all its beautiful colours!

never felt so deeply the blessing of a hospitable welcome and a warm fire. The man of the house repeated from time to time that we should often tell of this night when we got to our homes, and interposed praises of this, his own lake, which he had more than once, when we were returning in the boat, ventured to say was 'bonnier than Loch Lomond'. ·

Our companion from the Trossachs, who it appeared was an Edinburgh drawing-master going during the vacation on a pedestrian tour to John o' Groat's House, was to sleep in the barn with William and Coleridge, where the man said he had plenty of dry hay. I do not believe that the hay of the Highlands is often very dry, but this year it had a better chance than usual: wet or dry, however, the next morning they said they had slept comfortably. When I went to bed, the mistress, desiring me to 'go ben', attended me with a candle, and assured me that the bed was dry, though not 'sic as I had been used to'. It was of chaff; there were two others in the room, a cupboard and two chests, on one of which stood the milk in wooden vessels covered over; I should have thought that milk so kept could not have been sweet, but the cheese and butter were good. The walls of the whole house were of stone unplastered. It consisted of three apartments – the cow-house at one end, the kitchen or house in the middle, and the spence at the other end. The rooms were divided, not up to the rigging, but only to the beginning of the roof, so that there was a free passage for light and smoke from

The Rainbow

BY D. H. LAWRENCE (1885-1930)

Lawrence was born in Nottinghamshire, the son of a miner, and became a schoolteacher. His growing reputation as a writer encouraged him to devote himself to literature

Even the rainbow has a body
made of the drizzling rain
and is an architecture of glistening atoms
built up, built up
yet you can't lay your hand on it,
nay, nor even your mind.

'Landscape with a Rainbow' (near Chesterfield, Derbyshire, c 1795) by Joseph Wright of Derby (1734-97); oils. (*Derby Museum and Art Gallery*)

Cricket on a Sunday

BY CHARLES DICKENS (1812-70)

The following extract is from Part III – 'As It Might Be Made' – of *Sunday Under Three Heads* **by Charles Dickens. One of the author's lesser-known journalistic productions, it first appeared in wrappers, in 1836, when he was twenty-four, and was included in** *Reprinted Pieces* **when the Oxford University Press published** *The Uncommercial Traveller and Reprinted Pieces* **in 1958. Dickens wrote the piece to express his emancipated view that Sunday Observance attitudes should be more relaxed and tolerant**

I WAS travelling in the west of England a summer or two back, and was induced by the beauty of the scenery, and the seclusion of the spot, to remain for the night in a small village, distant about seventy miles from London. The next morning was Sunday; and I walked out towards the church. Groups of people – the whole population of the little hamlet apparently – were hastening in the same direction. Cheerful and good-humoured congratulations were heard on all sides, as neighbours overtook each other, and walked on in company. Occasionally I passed an aged couple, whose married daughter and her husband were loitering by the side of the old people, accommodating their rate of walking to their feeble pace, while a little knot of children hurried on before: stout young labourers in clean round frocks; and buxom girls with healthy, laughing faces were plentifully sprinkled about in couples, and the whole scene was one of quiet and tranquil contentment, irresistibly captivating. The morning was bright and pleasant, the hedges were green and blooming, and a thousand delicious scents were wafted on the air, from the wild flowers which blossomed on either side of the footpath. The little church was one of those venerable simple buildings which abound in the English counties; half-overgrown with moss and ivy, and standing in the centre of a little plot of ground, which, but for the green mounds with which it was studded, might have passed for a lovely meadow. I fancied that the old clanking bell which was now summoning the congregation together, would seem less terrible when it rung out the knell of a departed soul, than I had ever deemed possible before – that the sound would tell only of a welcome to calmness and rest, amidst the most peaceful and tranquil scene in nature.

Landscape with a church and beech-trees by Myles Birket Foster. (*The British Library, London*)

I followed into the church – a low-roofed building with small arched windows, through which the sun's rays streamed upon a plain tablet on the opposite wall, which had once recorded names, now as undistinguishable on its worn surface, as were the bones beneath, from the dust into which they had resolved. The impressive service of the Church of England was spoken – not merely *read* – by a grey-headed minister, and the responses delivered by his auditors, with an air of sincere devotion as far removed from affectation or display, as from coldness or indifference. The psalms were accompanied by a few instrumental performers, who were stationed in a small gallery extending across the church at the lower end, over the door: and the voices were led by the clerk, who it was evident derived no slight pride and gratification from this portion of the service. The discourse was plain, unpretending, and well adapted to the comprehension of the hearers. At the conclusion of the service, the villagers waited in the churchyard to salute the clergyman as he passed; and two or three, I observed, stepped aside, as if communicating some little difficulty, and asking his advice. This, to guess from the homely bows, and other rustic expressions of gratitude, the old gentleman readily conceded. He seemed intimately acquainted with the circumstances of all his parishioners; for I heard him inquire after one man's youngest child, another man's wife, and so forth; and that he was fond of his joke, I discovered from overhearing him ask a stout, fresh-coloured young fellow, with a very pretty bashful-looking girl on his arm, 'when those banns were to be put up?' – an inquiry which made the young fellow more fresh-coloured, and the girl more bashful, and which, strange to say, caused a great many other girls who were standing round, to colour up also, and look anywhere but in the faces of their male companions.

As I approached this spot in the evening about half an hour before sunset, I was surprised to hear the hum of voices, and occasionally a shout of merriment from the meadow beyond the church-yard; which I found, when I reached the stile, to be occasioned by a very animated game of cricket, in which the boys and young men of the place were engaged, while the females and old people were scattered about: some seated on the grass watching the progress of the game, and others sauntering about in groups of two or three, gathering little nosegays of wild roses and hedge flowers. I could not but take notice of one old man in particular, with a bright-eyed grand-daughter by his side, who was giving a sunburnt young fellow some instructions in the game, which he received with an air of profound deference, but with an occasional glance at the girl, which induced me to think that his attention was rather distracted from the old gentleman's narration of the fruits of his experience. When it was his turn at the wicket, too, there was a glance towards the pair every now and then, which the old grandfather very compla-cently considered as an appeal to his judgement of a particular hit, but which a certain blush in the girl's face, and a downcast look of the bright eye, led me to believe was intended for somebody else than the old man – and understood by somebody else, too, or I am much mistaken.

I was in the very height of the pleasure which the contemplation of this scene afforded me, when I saw the old clergy-man making his way towards us. I trembled for an angry interruption to the sport, and was almost on the point of crying out, to warn the cricketers of his approach; he was so close upon me, however, that I could do nothing but remain still, and anticipate the reproof that was preparing. What was my agreeable surprise to see the old gentleman standing at the stile, with his hands in his pockets, surveying the whole scene with evident satisfaction! And how dull I must have been, not to have known till my friend the grandfather (who, by the bye, said he had been a wonderful cricketer in his time) told me, that it was the clergyman himself who had established the whole thing: that it was his field they played in; and that it was he who had purchased stumps, bats, ball, and all!

It is such scenes as this I would see near London on a Sunday evening. It is such men as this who would do more in one year to make people properly religious, cheerful, and contented, than all the legislation of a century could ever accomplish.

'A Country Cricket Match, Sussex, 1878' by John R. Reid (1851-1926); oils.
(*The Tate Gallery, London*)

Stiles

BY RICHARD JEFFERIES (1848-87)

From *Wild Life in a Southern County*, **Wiltshire-born Richard Jefferies's book published in 1879**

EACH field has its characteristic stile – or rather two, one each side (at the entrance and exit of the footpath), and these are never alike. Walking across the fields for a couple of miles or more, of all the stiles that must of necessity be surmounted no two are similar. Here is one well put together – not too high, the rail not too large, and apparently an ideal piece of workmanship; but on approaching, the ground on the opposite side drops suddenly three or four feet – at the bottom is a marshy spot crossed by a narrow bridge of a single stone, on which you have to be careful to alight, or else plunge ankle-deep in water. If clever enough to drop on the stone, it immediately tilts up slightly, it is balanced somewhere, and has a see-saw motion well calculated to land the timid in the ditch.

The next is approached by a line of stepping-stones – to avoid the mud and water – whose surfaces are so irregular as barely to afford a footing. The stile itself is nothing – very low and easy to pass; but just beyond it a stiff, stout pole has been placed across to prevent horses straying, and below that a couple of hurdles are pitched to confine the sheep. This is almost too much; however, by patience and exertion, it is managed. Then comes a double mound with two stiles – one for each ditch – made very high and intended for steps; but the steps are worn away, and it is something like climbing a perpendicular ladder. Another has a toprail of a whole tree, so broad and thick no one can possibly straddle it, so some friend of humanity has broken the second rail, and you creep under. Finally comes a steep bank, six or seven feet high, with rude steps formed of the roots of trees worn bare by iron-tipped boots, and of mere holes in which to put the toe. At the top the stile leans forward over the precipice, so that you have to suspend yourself in mid-air. Fortunately, almost every other one has a gap worn at the side just large enough to squeeze through after coaxing the briars to yield a trifle. For it is intensely characteristic of human nature to make gaps and short cuts.

A stile worth lingering by, which appears to have none of the hazards mentioned by Richard Jefferies. Drawn by William Small for *The Quiver*, January 1871. (*The British Library, London*)

An idyllic woodland scene which, in spite of the detailed realism of the woodland plants and mossy stones, has a dream-like quality. (*A privately owned Victorian print; artist unknown*)

The Heron

BY PETER JONES (born 1929)

It stands on one leg
head-hunched, with no poise
of secret attraction, no eye·
of mystery to hypnotise eel
or mouse.

Equivocal serenity,
that takes in the marsh's
complaisant track, covering
the journey to the shallows.

The heron is still
and stays so;
until plumed lightning strikes
from its endless patience.

The British Library, London

The Water Babies

BY CHARLES KINGSLEY (1819-75)

Descriptive of moorland countryside in the north of England, this excerpt is taken from the Revd Charles Kingsley's book *The Water Babies.* **He wrote it chiefly for children, but it also has great appeal for adults, like his other famous title,** *Hereward the Wake*

AND now Tom was right away into the heather, and it grew more and more broken and hilly, but not so rough but that little Tom could jog along well enough, and find time, too, to stare about at the strange place, which was like a new world to him.

He saw great spiders there, with crowns and crosses marked on their backs, who sat in the middle of their webs, and when they saw Tom coming, shook them so fast that they became invisible. Then he saw lizards, brown and grey and green, and thought they were snakes, and would sting him; but they were as much frightened as he, and shot away into the heath. And then, under a rock, he saw a pretty sight – a great brown, sharp-nosed creature, with a white tag on her brush, and round her four or five smutty little cubs, the funniest fellows Tom ever saw. She lay on her back, rolling about, and stretching out her legs and head and tail in the bright sunshine; and the cubs jumped over her, and ran round her, and nibbled her paws, and lugged her about by the tail; and she seemed to enjoy it mightily. But one selfish little fellow stole away from the rest to a dead crow close by, and dragged it off to hide it, though it was nearly as big as he was. Whereat all his little brothers set off after him in full cry, and saw Tom; and then all ran back, and up jumped Mrs Vixen, and caught one up in her mouth, and the rest toddled after her, and into a dark crack in the rocks; and there was an end of the show.

And next he had a fright; for, as he scrambled up a sandy brow – whirr-poof-poof-cock-cock-kick – something went off in his face, with a most horrid noise. He thought the ground had blown up, and the end of the world come.

And when he opened his eyes (for he shut them very tight) it was only an old cock grouse, who had been washing himself in sand, like an Arab, for want of water; and who, when Tom had all but trodden on him, jumped up with a noise like the express train, leaving his wife and children to shift for themselves, like an old coward, and went off, screaming 'Cur-ru-u-uck, cur-ru-u-uck – murder,

thieves, fire – cur-u-cuk-cock-kick – the spiders, go and catch spiders – kick.'
end of the world is come – kick-kick-cock-kick.' He was always fancying that the end of the world was come, when anything happened which was farther off than the end of his own nose. But the end of the world was not come, any more than the twelfth of August was; though the old grouse cock was quite certain of it.

So the old grouse came back to his wife and family an hour afterwards, and said solemnly, 'Cock-cock-kick; my dears, the end of the world is not quite come; but I assure you it is coming the day after tomorrow – cock.' But his wife had heard that so often that she knew all about it, and a little more. And, besides, she was the mother of a family, and had seven little poults to wash and feed every day; and that made her very practical, and a little sharp-tempered; so all she answered was 'Kick-kick-kick – go and catch

So Tom went on and on, he hardly knew why, but he liked the great wide strange place, and the cool fresh bracing air. But he went more and more slowly as he got higher up the hill; for now the ground grew very bad indeed. Instead of soft turf and springy heather, he met great patches of flat limestone rock, just like ill-made pavements, with deep cracks between the stones and ledges, filled with ferns; so he had to hop from stone to stone, and now and then he slipped in between, and hurt his little bare toes, though they were tolerably tough ones; but still he would go on and up, he could not tell why.

And now he began to get a little hungry, and very thirsty; for he had run a long way, and the sun had risen high in heaven, and the rock was as hot as an oven, and the air danced reels over it, as

it does over a limekiln, till everything round seemed quivering and melting in the glare.

But he could see nothing to eat anywhere, and still less to drink.

The heath was full of bilberries and whinberries; but they were only in flower yet, for it was June. And as for water, who can find that on the top of a limestone rock? Now and then he passed by a deep dark swallow-hole, going down into the earth, as if it was the chimney of some dwarf's house underground; and more than once, as he passed, he could hear water falling, trickling, tinkling, many many feet below. How he longed to get down to it, and cool his poor baked lips! But, brave little chimney-sweep as he was, he dared not climb down such chimneys as those.

So he went on and on, till his head spun round with the heat, and he thought he heard churchbells ringing a long way off.

'Ah!' he thought, 'where there is a church there will be houses and people; and, perhaps, someone will give me a bit and a sup.' So he set off again, to look for the church; for he was sure that he heard the bells quite plain.

And in a minute more, when he looked round, he stopped again, and said, 'Why, what a big place the world is!'

And so it was; for, from the top of the mountain he could see – what could he not see?

Behind him, far below, was Harthover, and the dark woods, and the shining salmon river; and on his left, far below, was the town, and the smoking chimneys of the collieries; and far, far away, the river widened to the shining sea; and little white specks, which were ships, lay on its bosom. Before him lay, spread out like a map, great plains, and farms, and villages, amid dark knots of trees. They all seemed at his very feet; but he had sense to see that they were long miles away.

And to his right rose moor after moor, hill after hill, till they faded away, blue into blue sky. But between him and those moors, and really at his very feet, lay something to which, as soon as Tom saw it, he determined to go, for that was the place for him.

A deep, deep green and rocky valley, very narrow, and filled with wood; but through the wood, hundreds of feet below him, he could see a clear stream glance. Oh, if he could but get down to that stream! Then, by the stream, he saw the roof of a little cottage, and a little garden set out in squares and beds. And there was a tiny red thing moving in the garden, no bigger than a fly. As Tom looked down, he saw that it was a woman in a red petticoat. Ah! perhaps she would give him something to eat. And there were the churchbells ringing again. Surely there must be a village down there. Well, nobody would know him, or what had happened at the Place. The news could not have got there yet, even if Sir John had set all the policemen in the county after him; and he could get down there in five minutes.

Tom was quite right about the hue and cry not having got thither; for he had come, without knowing it, the best part of ten miles from Harthover; but he was wrong about getting down in five minutes, for the cottage was more than a mile off, and a good thousand feet below.

However, down he went, like a brave little man as he was, though he was very footsore, and tired, and hungry, and thirsty; while the churchbells rang so loud, he began to think that they must be inside his own head, and the river  chimed and tinkled far below; and this was the song which it sang:

> Clear and cool, clear and cool,
> By laughing shallow, and dreaming
>   pool;
>   Cool and clear, cool and clear,
> By shining shingle, and foaming wear;
> Under the crag where the ouzel sings,
> And the ivied wall where the churchbell
>   rings,
>   Undefiled, for the undefiled;
> Play by me, bathe in me, mother
>   and child.
>
> Dank and foul, dank and foul,
> By the smoky town in its murky cowl;
>   Foul and dank, foul and dank,
> By wharf and sewer and slimy bank;
> Darker and darker the farther I go,

Baser and baser the richer I grow;
  Who dare sport with the sin-
    defiled?
  Shrink from me, turn from me,
    mother and child.

> Strong and free, strong and free,
> The floodgates are open, away to the
>   sea,
>   Free and strong, free and strong,
>   Cleansing my streams as I hurry along,
> To the golden sands, and the leaping
>   bar,
> And the taintless tide that awaits me
>   afar.
> As I lose myself in the infinite main,
> Like a soul that has sinned and is
>   pardoned again.
>   Undefiled, for the undefiled;
>   Play by me, bathe in me, mother
>   and child.

Tramps

BY CHARLES DICKENS (1812-70)

Like 'Cricket on a Sunday', this piece is drawn from *The Uncommercial Traveller and Reprinted Pieces.* **Dickens describes the various types of tramp frequenting the roads in the middle of the 19th century**

ANOTHER class of tramp is a man, the most valuable part of whose stock-in-trade is a highly perplexed demeanour. He is got up like a countryman, and you will often come upon the poor fellow, while he is endeavouring to decipher the inscription on a milestone – quite a fruitless endeavour, for he cannot read. He asks your pardon, he truly does (he is very slow of speech, this tramp, and he looks in a bewildered way all round the prospect while he talks to you), but all of us shold do as we wold be done by, and he'll take it kind, if you'll put a power man in the right road fur to jine his eldest son as has broke his leg bad in the masoning, and is in this heere Orspit'l as is wrote down by Squire Pouncerby's own hand as wold not tell a lie fur no man. He then produces from under his dark frock (being always very slow and perplexed) a neat but worn old leathern purse, from which he takes a scrap of paper. On this scrap of paper is written, by Squire Pouncerby, of The Grove, 'Please to direct the Bearer, a poor but very worthy man, to the Sussex County Hospital, near Brighton' – a matter of some difficulty at the moment, seeing that the request comes suddenly upon you in the depths of Hertfordshire. The more you endeavour to indicate where Brighton is – when you have with the greatest difficulty remembered – the less the devoted father can be made to comprehend, and the more obtusely he stares at the prospect; whereby, being

Figures for Landscapes, drawn and etched by W. H. Pyne, published 1812.
(*Radio Times Hulton Picture Library*)

The Chairmender, an illustration from Tom Taylor's *Pictures of an English Landscape* (1862) by Myles Birket Foster (1825-99). (*The British Library, London*)

Ploughmen, drawn and etched by W. H. Pyne, published 1802.
(*Radio Times Hulton Picture Library*)

reduced to extremity, you recommend the faithful parent to begin by going to St Albans, and present him with half-a-crown. It does him good, no doubt, but scarcely helps him forward, since you find him lying drunk that same evening in the wheelwright's sawpit under the shed where the felled trees are, opposite the sign of the Three Jolly Hedgers.

But, the most vicious, by far, of all the idle tramps, is the tramp who pretends to have been a gentleman. 'Educated,' he writes, from the village beer-shop in pale ink of a ferruginous complexion; 'educated at Trin Coll Cam – nursed in the lap of affluence – once in my small way the pattron of the Muses,' &c &c &c – surely a sympathetic mind will not withhold a trifle, to help him on to the market town where he thinks of giving a Lecture to the *fruges consumere nati*, on things in general? This shameful creature lolling about hedge taprooms in his ragged clothes, now so far from being black that they look as if they never can have been black, is more selfish and insolent than even the savage tramp. He would sponge on the poorest boy for a farthing, and spurn him when he had got it; he would interpose (if he could get anything by it) between the baby and the mother's breast. So much lower than the company he keeps, for his maudlin assumption of being higher, this pitiless rascal blights the summer road as he maunders on between the luxuriant hedges; where (to my thinking) even the wild convolvulus and rose and sweetbriar are the worse for his going by, and need time to recover from the taint of him in the air.

The young fellows who trudge along barefoot, five or six together, their boots slung over their shoulders, their shabby bundles under their arms, their sticks newly cut from some roadside wood, are not eminently prepossessing, but are much less objectionable. There is a tramp-fellowship among them. They pick one another up at resting stations, and go on in companies. They always go at a fast swing – though they generally limp too – and there is invariably one of the company who has much ado to keep up with the rest. They generally talk about horses, and any other means of locomotion than walking: or, one of the company relates some recent experiences of the road – which are always disputes and difficulties. As for example. 'So as I'm a  red once more. By that time, we should standing at the pump in the market, blest have ground our way to the sea cliffs, and if there don't come up a Beadle, and he the whirr of our wheel would be lost in ses, "Mustn't stand here," he ses. "Why the breaking of the waves. Our next not?" I ses. "No beggars allowed in this variety in sparks would be derived from town," he ses. "Who's a beggar?" I ses. contrast with the gorgeous medley of "You are," he ses. "Who ever see *me* colours in the autumn woods, and, by beg? Did *you*?" I ses. "Then you're a the time we had ground our way round to tramp," he ses. "I'd rather be that than the heathy lands between Reigate and a Beadle," I ses.' (The company express Croydon, doing a prosperous stroke of great approval.) ' "Would you?" he ses to business all along, we should show like a me. "Yes, I would," I ses to him. "Well," little firework in the light frosty air, and he ses, "anyhow, get out of this town." be the next best thing to the blacksmith's "Why, blow your little town!" I ses, forge. Very agreeable, too, to go on a "who wants to be in it? Wot does your chair-mending tour. What judges · we dirty little town mean by comin' and should be of rushes and how knowingly stickin' itself in the road to anywhere? (with a sheaf and a bottomless chair at Why don't you get a shovel and a barrer, our back) we should lounge on bridges, and clear your town out o' people's looking over at osier-beds! Among all the way?" ' (The company expressing the innumerable occupations that cannot highest approval and laughing aloud, possibly be transacted without the assis- they all go down the hill.) tance of lookers-on, chair-mending may

Then, there are the tramp handicraft take a station in the first rank. When we men. Are they not all over England, in sat down with our backs against the barn this midsummer time? Where does the or the public house, and began to mend, lark sing, the corn grow, the mill turn, what a sense of popularity would grow the river run, and they are not among the upon us! When all the children came to lights and shadows, tinkering, chair- look at us, and the tailor, and the general mending, umbrella-mending, clock- dealer, and the farmer who had been mending, knife-grinding? Surely, a giving a small order at the little saddler's, pleasant thing, if we were in that condi- and the groom from the great house, and tion of life, to grind our way through the publican, and even the two skittle Kent, Sussex, and Surrey. For the worst players (and here note that, howsoever six weeks or so, we should see the sparks busy all the rest of village human-kind we ground off, fiery bright against a may be, there will always be two people background of green wheat and green with leisure to play at skittles, wherever leaves. A little later, and the ripe harvest village skittles are), what encouragement would pale our sparks from red to yellow, would be on us to plait and weave! No until we got the dark newly-turned land one looks at us while we plait and weave for a background again, and they were these words.

Summer's End

BY THOMAS HARDY (1840-1928)

It was a morning of the latter summer-time; a morning of lingering dews, when the grass is never dry in the shade. Fuchsias and dahlias were laden till eleven o'clock with small drops and dashes of water, changing the colour of their sparkle at every movement of the air; and elsewhere hanging on twigs like small silver fruit. The threads of garden-spiders appeared thick and polished. In the dry and sunny places dozens of long-legged crane-flies whizzed off the grass at every step the passer took.

The British Library, London

The Harvest Field

BY ROBERT BLOOMFIELD (1768-1823)

Robert Bloomfield, like the poet John Clare,
was an agricultural labourer who became an
author in the face of difficulties and used his
Suffolk background as the theme of his poetry

Here, 'midst the boldest triumphs of her worth,
Nature herself invites the reapers forth;
Dares the keen sickle from its twelvemonths' rest,
And gives that ardour which in every breast
From infancy to age alike appears,
When the first sheaf its plumy top uprears.
No rake takes here what Heaven to all bestows —
Children of want, for you the bounty flows!
And every cottage from the plenteous store
Receives a burden nightly at its door.
   Hark! where the sweeping scythe now rips
      along:
Each sturdy mower emulous and strong;
Whose writhing form meridian heat defies,
Bends o'er his work, and every sinew tries;
Prostrates the waving treasure at his feet,
But spares the rising clover, short and sweet.
Come, Health! come, Jollity! light-footed, come;
Here hold your revels, and make this your home.
Each heart awaits and hails you as its own;
Each moisten'd brow, that scorns to wear a frown:
Th' unpeopled dwelling mourns its tenants stray'd;
E'en the domestic laughing dairymaid
Hies to the field, the general toil to share.
Meanwhile the Farmer quits his elbow-chair,

His cool brick floor, his pitcher, and his ease,
And braves the sultry beams, and gladly sees
His gates thrown open, and his team abroad,
The ready group attendant on his word,
To turn the swarth, the quiv'ring load to rear,
Or ply the busy rake, the land to clear.
Summer's light garb itself now cumbrous grown,
Each his thin doublet in the shade throws down;
Where oft the mastiff skulks with half-shut eye,
And rouses at the stranger passing by;
Whilst unrestrain'd the social converse flows,
And every breast Love's powerful impulse knows,
And rival wits with more than rustic grace
Confess the presence of a pretty face.
   For, lo! encircled there, the lovely Maid,
In youth's own bloom and native smiles array'd;
Her hat awry, divested of her gown,
Her creaking stays of leather, stout and brown;
Invidious barrier! why art thou so high,
When the slight covering of her neck slips by,
There half-revealing to the eager sight
Her full, ripe bosom, exquisitely white?
In many a local tale of harmless mirth,
And many a jest of momentary birth,
She bears a part, and, as she stops to speak,
Strokes back the ringlets from her glowing cheek.
   Now noon gone by, and four declining hours,
The weary limbs relax their boasted pow'rs;
Thirst rages strong, the fainting spirits fail,
And ask the sov'reign cordial, home-brew'd ale:
Beneath some shelt'ring heap of yellow corn
Rests the hoop'd keg, and friendly cooling horn,
That mocks alike the goblet's brittle frame,
Its costlier potions, and its nobler name.
To *Mary* first the brimming draught is given,
By toil made welcome as the dews of heaven,
And never lip that press'd its homely edge
Had kinder blessings or a heartier pledge.

'The Harvest Waggon' by Francis Wheatley (1747-1801); oils.
(Castle Museum and Art Gallery, Nottingham. Photograph: Layland-Ross Ltd.)

The Thatcher

BY RICHARD JEFFERIES (1848-87)

Thatch was once the cheapest material for covering houses, barns, cattlesheds and ricks, and gave protection against the cold of winter and heat of summer alike. Reeds, or the very best hand-cut wheat straw, were used. Nowadays, with modern roof-coverings cheaper and easier to apply, few thatchers are to be found

A MAN of no little consequence is the thatcher, the most important perhaps of the hamlet craftsmen. He ornaments the wheat ricks with curious twisted tufts of straw, standing up not unlike the fantastic ways in which savages are represented doing their hair. But he does not put the thatch on the wheat half so substantially as formerly, because now only a few remain the winter – the thatch is often hardly on before it is off again for the thrashing-machine – for the 'sheening', as they call it. On the hayricks, which stand longer, he puts better work, especially on the southern and western sides or angles, binding it down with a crosswork of bonds to prevent the gales which blow from those quarters unroofing the rick.

It is said to be an ill wind that blows nobody any good: now the wind never blew that was strong enough to please the thatcher. If the hurricane roughs up the straw on all the ricks in the parish, unroofs half a dozen sheds, and does not spare the gables of the dwelling-houses, why, he has work for the next two months. He is attended by a man to carry up the 'yelms,' and two or three women are busy 'yelming' – i.e. separating the straw, selecting the longest and laying it level and parallel, damping it with water, and preparing it for the yokes. These yokes must be cut from boughs that have grown naturally in the shape wanted, else they are not tough enough. A tough old chap, too, is the thatcher, a man of infinite gossip, well acquainted with the genealogy of every farmer, and, indeed, of everybody from Dan to Beersheba, of the parish.

Thatching a barn. This picture appeared in the *Illustrated London News*, 3 October 1846. (*Radio Times Hulton Picture Library*)

'Reapers' Noonday Rest' by John Linnell (1792-1882); oils. (*The Tate Gallery, London*)

Rickmaking

BY RICHARD JEFFERIES (1848-87)

Few hay-ricks are to be seen now; mechanised farming has altered everything. Square-shaped bundles of hay are stacked in an open-sided Dutch barn, probably topped with a corrugated-iron roof; or else they are stored under plastic sheeting, possibly weighted down by heavy rubber tyres

NOTHING is done right now, according to the old men of the hamlet; even the hayricks are built badly and 'scamped'. The rickmaker used to be an important person, generally a veteran, who had to be conciliated with an extra drop of good liquor before he could be got to set to work in earnest. Then he spread the hay here, and worked it in there, and had it trodden down at the edge, and then in the middle, and, like the centurion, sent men hither and thither. His rick, when complete, did not rise perpendicularly, but each face or square side sloped a little outwards – including the ends – a method that certainly does give the rick a very shapely look.

But now the new-fangled 'elevator' carries up the hay by machinery from the wagon to the top, and two ricks are run up while they would formerly have just been carefully laying the foundation for one of faggots to keep off the damp. The poles put up to support the rick-cloth interfere with the mathematically correct outward slope at the ends, upon which the old fellow prided himself; so they are carried up straight like the end wall of a cottage, and are a constant source of contempt to the ancient invalid. However, he consoles himself with the reflection that most of the men employed with the 'elevator' will ultimately go to a very unpleasant place, since they are continuously swearing at the horse that works it, to make him go round the faster.

Hop-pickers, about 1857. From *Grundy's English Views* – taken by a Mr Grundy, of Birmingham. (*Radio Times Hulton Picture Library*)

Filling sacks with the hops; the hop-poles are now bare: c 1900. (*Radio Times Hulton Picture Library*)

Hop Picking

BY EDMUND BLUNDEN (1896-1974)

The poet and critic Edmund Blunden was born
in the Weald of Kent, fought in the First
World War and was badly gassed. Most of his
life was spent as a university teacher; from
1966 to 1968 he was Professor of Poetry at
Oxford. Much of his poetry is inspired by the
Kent countryside which he loved

The hoptime came with sun and shower
That made the hops hang hale and good;
The village swarmed with motley folk,
For through the morning calm awoke
Noise of the toiling multitude
Who stripped the tall bines' bower.

Slatternly folk from sombre streets
And crowded courts like narrow wells
Are picking in that fragrant air;
Gypsies with jewelled fingers there
Gaze dark, speak low; their manner tells
Of thievings and deceits.

And country dames with mittened wrists,
Grandams and girls and mothers stand
And stretch the bine-head on the bin,
And deftly jerk the loosed hops in.
Black stains the never-resting hand
So white for springtide trysts.

And by and by the little boys,

Tired with the work and women's talk,
Make slyly off, and run at large
Down to the river, board the barge
Roped in to shore, and stand to baulk
The bargee's angry noise:

While through the avenues of hops
The measurers and the poke-boys go.
The measurers scoop the heaped hops out,
While gaitered binmen move about
With sharpened hopdog, at whose blow
The stubborn cluster drops.

Such was the scene that autumn morn,
But when the drier in his oast
Had loaded up his lattice-floors,
He called a binman at the doors,
'We want no more; the kilns are closed.
Bid measurers blow the horn.'

The binman found the measurer pleased,
For hops were clean and work was through;
He told him what the drier said,
The measurer nodded his grey head,
Lifted the battered horn and blew.
And so the day's work ceased.

The Forge

FROM *AKENFIELD* BY RONALD BLYTHE

Akenfield is the name given by Ronald Blythe to a village in East Anglia and to his book about that village and its inhabitants and their lives and customs. Ronald Blythe was born in a village in Suffolk and returned to live in East Anglia on becoming a full-time writer in 1955. *Akenfield,* **first published in 1969, is widely judged to be a modern classic among country books**

IT was all agricultural work at the forge. Mostly shoeing. All the horses were still with us and at seventeen I was shoeing an average of eight horses a day. I remember making my first horse-shoe. I started work at the forge on August 2nd and I made this shoe on August 4th. They put you straight into the collar in those days! There was no messing about. When you got a job you began doing it right away. You were expected to catch on quick.

The man my grandmother allowed to run the forge was old and when I was just over seventeen he retired, and I had to carry on alone. I now had to do every mortal thing myself. What I didn't know I had to find out or make up. There was nobody to ask. It was a terrible job, but there, we got over it. It was still all farm work, of course. Mostly shoeing. The horseman would stand at the head while the work was being done, so that was a bit of help. He could hold it like. I was such a thin little lad it was a masterpiece how I could hold anything! There was no thought of what you might call art-and-craft work, only plough coulters, harrows, door-hinges and such farm things. There was no money about; everybody was bare-poor. I charged 6s 8d to put four shoes on a horse. I reckoned that with a quiet horse with good feet the task would take an hour. I hardly made a profit. There are still plenty of horses round here, of course – hunt horses, pony-club horses – it is most unusual for a village to have so many of them around. And I don't mind shoeing them. The trouble is that people who have these kind of horses reckon on you shoeing them for next to nothing. I won't do that. Not now. If people will pay what I charge and won't grumble, then I'll shoe for them, but not otherwise. I am supposed to have served a five-year apprenticeship, and if work isn't worth a little when you've done that, then blast them. I won't mess after it. I remember how hard it was to make myself free, for that is what I was really up to when I was here all alone before the war. I don't know what it is, I can't explain it, but you see I am the only one out of all my family – and there are five of us brothers – who had any intention of coming to the smithy. My brothers couldn't have cared less about the place. I wanted to come, *had* to come. But it is silly to be sentimental. What I sometimes think is that I am my grandfather, an old one. It is the truth when I say that I can sit in the shop of a Sunday, smoking my pipe, and be as happy as if I were sitting in the house. I wasn't born soon enough, that is the trouble. By rights, I should be dead and gone. I think like the old people. I have a tendency to do what I want to do, if the maggot bites. However pressing matters are, I do what I fancy. I think, probably, my attitude could be wrong. We have our pressures now with bills and bank managers and book-keeping, but I say to myself, this is not the highest thing; this is business. You are a tradesman; this is the highest thing. Making, doing. I feel I should have lived during the 1700s. That would have done me. But I am losing my place, aren't I?

Well, the war came, and one or two German prisoners came to help me out. They were pleasant lads. When they went back I had a boy from the army school, after he had finished his training. He had been an army apprentice farrier and I finished him off. When he left, one or two more arrived and for the first time in my life I had a few minutes to spare, so I began to amuse myself by making ornamental things. I entered one or two competitions and won prizes. And then, after the war, this wonderful thing happened, I married. The business was steady now. I had over a hundred horses on my books which had to be shod three times a year, which meant that I was making 1,200 shoes a year. Of course, the horses were passing, but so slowly that it didn't seem possible that they were soon to disappear off the farms for ever. I still saw the things I sent to the crafts section of the Suffolk Show as a hobby – I couldn't imagine living by such work.

Then new people came and bought up the old houses. They'd spend a mint of money 'putting it all back as it was'. They couldn't buy the things they needed for the restoration; they hadn't been made for donkey's years. So I had to start making them again. My wife went round, keeping her eye open for bolts, latches, handles, grates; drawing them and finding out their dates, and I made more of them as exactly as you're not likely to tell the difference. Mind you, it took time. It took all hours. But it was a fine thing for me to have something lying on the bench before me made by one of the old men, and my hands doing again what his had done. The new business grew and grew. The Trust House people had bought the Suffolk coaching-houses and now they were doing them up regardless. They wanted to do everything in the old-fashioned way, all mortise-and-tenon studs and plaster. And, of course, handmade nails. I made all the nails they used. They were each forged and hammered from the hot spar. And they were expensive, I can tell you. You can buy a pound of ordinary machine-made nails for 9d but mine cost 4½d each. A strange thing happened while I was hammering these nails. They found a great pile of Roman nails in the Scottish mountains, all as bright as if they had been made yesterday. I could quite understand why this was because these nails would have been made from lowmoor which doesn't rust.

It is steel which rusts. Do you know what I thought when I heard of these great Roman nails? – those would have been like the nails they would have used for the Crucifixion. They would have been made from iron smelted with charcoal. This is why the Swedish iron is so good because they were using charcoal right up to my day. But you can't buy iron now; it is all steel. They will smelt it especially for you if you order ten tons of it, but charge you a ridiculous price.

We have to make do with mild steel for all our work, and this is why you get all this trouble with agricultural things breaking sudden like. These steels are too strong. They cannot give. They just get fatigue and snap. They are too good for rough purposes – if you can call anything too good. Iron would do the job much better. But then you can't electric-weld iron. It has to be fire-welded. That is why they manufacture mild steel to fit in with modern methods of production. It is not easier to work – oh no! It is simply easier to weld because you are using electricity and not fire. But iron is always better for bending and real forging. The various parts of the new agricultural machines are all profiled out in the gas-flame; they are cut out flat, not bent. All this has happened during the last few years, so everything is different. We've got a profile machine which cuts the pattern out in a piece of tin. You screw it in on top, light the gas – propane and oxygen – and work with a cutting-head with an electric motor and a magnet attached to it. This runs around your plate and carves out its shape in the metal below. Ours will cut two inches thick. Before this method was invented everything at the smithy had to be forged and knocked into shape.

'A Blacksmith's Shop' by Joseph Wright of Derby (1734-97); oils.
(*Paul Mellon Collection, Yale Center for British Art*)

The Patchwork English Inn

BY RICHARD KEVERNE

Richard Keverne collected the material for his book *Tales of Old Inns* **(first published in 1939 and of which this extract is the introductory chapter) over a period of nearly twenty years – travelling along old coach roads, talking to landlords and 'oldest inhabitants', searching museums and records and covering more than a hundred inns in England and Wales**

YOU may take it that most half-timbered inns of any consequence originally had open galleries on two or three sides of a courtyard. There is an example at the George at Huntingdon. The guest chambers led from these galleries which were approached by outside staircases. As time went on they closed in these galleries as a protection against the weather and in this condition a surprising number of them remain.

An inn-yard is a happy hunting ground for relics of the past. All sorts of 'bygones' get stored away as lumber in its deserted buildings. The old loose boxes nowadays are turned into garages, but the harness rooms and ostlers' rooms are generally to be found. And in some corner of the yard there is often a discarded mounting-block used by our more portly forebears to help them into the saddle.

Above the stables in the bigger inns were the post-boys' quarters. The post-boy was a postilion who rode one of a pair of horses attached to a post-chaise. The traveller by chaise, a light carriage with a hood that could be opened, had perforce to change horses every few miles, generally ten to twelve or fifteen according to the condition of the road. This was a 'stage'. At each fresh stage a new pair and post-boy, or two pairs and two post-boys if the traveller were rich or in a hurry, were engaged. The first post-boy, when his horses were rested, would return with another chaise going to his inn. And since this posting trade was a very necessary and lucrative one, every posting inn had a large number of horses always ready, 'at call' as the phrase was, hence the vast stables that still remain.

Behind the inn-yard, seek the garden and the bowling-green. Most old inns had big kitchen gardens and bowling-greens, and fortunately both these features have frequently been maintained.

But the Brew Houses, another characteristic of the big inn-yard, have gone – out of use at any rate. You sometimes find them deserted and neglected, and see their copper utensils used for decoration in the public rooms of the inn.

The arch that leads to the yard has often a story to tell. Sometimes it has been heightened to admit the entrance of coaches. Often there are hooks left in its roof from which game and joints hung in a cooling breeze.

Look for the old kitchen just inside the archway, more often than not on the right. And in the kitchen look above the fireplaces for survivals of the racks that held the spits that pierced joints and birds in the days when they were roasted before an open fire, not baked in an oven. And look for relics of the roasting jacks that turned the spits. Sometimes you will find the jack complete though no longer in use.

The 'Long Room' was a Georgian convention. It was known by many names: the 'Great Room', the 'Big Room', the 'Assembly Room'. It is nearly always on the first floor with a window leading onto the top of the porch, the room of big functions, dinners and dances. It usually had a movable partition or folding doors so that it could be divided. Nowadays it is in use as dining-room or lounge, or broken up into several bedrooms. It usually had a fireplace of the same design at each end and an ante-chamber leading from it. So where the old 'Long Room' has been divided its former size may be traced by discovering the second fireplace, and if you examine the intervening walls the odds are they will prove to be mere partitions.

It was seldom that a really old inn was completely rebuilt in the Posting Era unless, it was burnt down. It was the front block to the street that was rebuilt or reconditioned to make a good modern show; so seek the older parts in the wings.

Old inns had a habit of changing their signs. As often as not the change was made by a new landlord who followed a bad one and sought to get rid of a sign that had acquired a bad name. Sometimes there was a political significance, sometimes it was purely arbitrary. The frequent change to the something 'Arms' was an affectation of refinement that began in the later 1700s and became more common in the next three or four decades. No really old inn first hung out the sign of somebody's arms, any more than it called itself an 'Hotel'. It was content to be known bluntly as the White Horse or the Star, the George or Red Lion Inn, and put out a bold sign for the information of a generation of which few could read.

Then there were Trade Tokens. They might be described as unofficial coins, halfpennies and farthings usually, issued by the leading traders in the middle 1600s. They were issued to provide small change of which there was a great lack at the time. Their issuers were men of standing who guaranteed to redeem their tokens in coin of the realm, and these tokens passed freely in circulation, not only in the towns of their issue, but for many miles around. The existence of an innkeeper's token is a very certain assurance that his inn at that time was of considerable importance.

As to the origin of the 'Coaching Clock' so often found in an old Posting House, there is some uncertainty. It is known also as the 'Inn Clock' and the 'Act of Parliament Clock'. The generally accepted

Outside a Village Inn, an illustration by Myles Birket Foster (1825-99) from Tom Taylor's
Pictures of an English Landscape (1862). (*The British Library, London*)

'Chill October' by Sir John Millais (1829-96); oils. (*On loan to Perth Museum and Art Gallery*)

explanation of the latter name is that this type of clock was introduced in 1797 when a tax was imposed upon private timepieces and many people gave up their own clocks. So the innkeeper provided a public clock for the convenience of his patrons. But the 'Coaching Clock' was in use before 1797. Other tales tell vaguely of a law which compelled landlords of coaching-inns to provide a standard clock for their houses. But the fact remains that they are of a distinctive type associated with inns. Their cases are nearly always plain, with a simple decoration on a black ground, and varnished. And we may take it that their reason for being was much the same as that of a clock in a railway station: that travellers might always know the correct time.

Of other characteristics of old inns perhaps the rarest is the chequered or lozenge sign of which possibly that at the Methuen Arms at Corsham is the only one left. It was the common sign of a tavern for centuries, and it probably has only survived at Corsham because it was painted on stone. On plaster or woodwork it would have been painted or whitewashed over years ago. So look for it in a stone country, on the doorposts of what was the chief bar entrance, not the main entrance to the inn. And if you ever happen on it, beg, bribe or threaten the landlord into preserving it.

You will find, as you study old inns, that they run very true to type. Their plan is as conventional as that of a church. But the plan is confused by later accretions. In seeking it out use detective methods, following up clues from room to room, watching the run of the main chimney, frequently the oldest part of the house, the base of which you may discover in an unaccountable sort of buttress in the cellar. Follow old moulded beams and cornices to ceilings and they will tell you of big rooms divided. It is the same with old tales, and traditions. Age has distorted them, but there is generally an ancient truth behind the garbled modern version. Read the tradition of the Plymouth Brethren at the Red Lion at Luton to exemplify this.

Patiently studying each patch in the jumbled fabric or tale you will find it joining up with another presently to make something of a whole to form a readable chapter of the inn's story.

They are still patching old inns, marking them as definitely with a tale of the second half of the twentieth century for future amateurs to read, as the 'Long Room' tells today of the last half of the eighteenth. They are closing up the archways to the yards to form entrance halls or lounges. The lover of old inns can but deplore it. But the inn must be practical. The archway was for the horse: that has gone. The motor car goes in by the back entrance to the yard to garage in an old loose box. So often, as at the Swan at Lavenham, the archway divided the house, and when it was no longer essential to the business of the inn, it became just an inconvenience. And the inn only survives, it must be remembered, where the landlords have adapted their houses to meet the changing needs of their patrons. But in many cases, like the one quoted, the old outline of the archway has been left, so that the general appearance of the inn has not been seriously altered.

That is the way an inn should be modernised. The architect must be a man who understands and has a feeling for old things, and so must the builder and

141

his workmen. To pull down and build afresh is so often the quickest and easiest thing to do, and so much less expensive. Because of this, a great many of our old inns have disappeared or been entirely bereft of their original character during this century. The policy of the owners of the inns varies. In some cases there is complete disregard for antiquity. The commercially-minded will often inform their builders that speed in the alterations is all they ask. Sometimes an attempt is made to conform in the renovations to the original structure, but the architect and builders have insufficient experience. In either case, the results are disastrous. But during the years before the war, there was a growing tendency to regard antiquity as an asset in a house, and, therefore, to preserve the old appearance even through drastic alterations. The public has passed through the stage in which everything had to be modern and chromium-plated and there has developed now a very widespread and genuine love for old things.

But the desire to maintain the old appearance of an inn must not be allowed to check its development. An inn is not a public monument, however old. And its charm is that it has reacted architecturally to the various periods of our history. If more travellers pass through a town, then the town's inns must expand. If travellers want lounges, and wash-basins in the bedrooms, then they must be provided, regardless of whether they fit in with the appearance of the inn as a 'period piece'. But in all these changes, whether expansion or alterations to make the inn more up to date, they should be made to conform to the old pattern of the inn and to preserve as much as possible of the original fabric of the house. This costs money and requires both patience and experience.

It is interesting what a wealth of fine, old work can be uncovered during renovations to these old inns. At Lavenham, for instance, the lovely, half-timbered front was concealed behind a flat façade, the gables of which were edged with plaster frills so that there was little indication from the outside of the place as it is today. The Bull at Long Melford was another; at one time the inn presented to the street a flat brick front with a stone coping. Behind was the old half-timbered face and the mellow tile roof that you see today. In renovations here, the half-timbering was exposed, but on the ground floor it was in such a bad state that it was not possible to retain the old structure. A new wall was, therefore, built after the style of the old, so that the inn retains its original appearance.

We must remember, whilst looking at these old inns, that they are commercial undertakings. They are adjusting themselves to the ever-changing needs of the times and they will go on adjusting themselves. If the public want old inns, then the old inns will be preserved. But if the public taste changes violently, then those old half-timbered houses will gradually disappear. That is the fascination of these old inns. They are essentially a patchwork, architecturally sympathetic to the public taste of each age they serve. That is how they survive and how they will continue to survive.

An Amusing Incident at a Country Inn

BY GEORGE BORROW (1803-81)

This episode is from *Wild Wales*, published in 1862. Famous as a life-long traveller who wrote of his experiences at home and abroad – not least among the gypsies – Borrow's account of his long walk through the Welsh countryside vividly depicts the life and landscape of Wales at that period

DESCENDING a hill, I came to a bridge under which ran a beautiful river, which came foaming down a gully between two of the eastern hills. From a man whom I met I learned that the bridge was called Pont Coomb Linau, and that the name of the village I had passed was Linau. The river carries an important tribute to the Dyfi, at least it did when I saw it, though perhaps in summer it is little more than a dry watercourse.

Half an hour's walking brought me from this place to a small town or large village, with a church at the entrance and the usual yew-tree in the churchyard. Seeing a kind of inn, I entered it and was shown by a lad-waiter into a large kitchen in which were several people. I had told him in Welsh that I wanted some ale, and as he opened the door he cried with a loud voice *Cumro!* as much as to say, Mind what you say before this chap, for he understands *Cumraeg* – that word

was enough. The people, who were talking fast and eagerly as I made my appearance, instantly became silent and stared at me with most suspicious looks. I sat down and when my ale was brought I took a hearty draught, and observing that the company were still watching me suspiciously and maintaining the same suspicious silence, I determined to comport myself in a manner which should to a certain extent afford them ground for suspicion. I therefore slowly and deliberately drew my notebook out of my waistcoat pocket, unclasped it, took my pencil from the loops at the side of the book, and forthwith began to dot down observations upon the room and company, now looking to the left, now to the right, now aloft, now alow, now skewing at an object, now leering at an individual, my eyes half-closed and my mouth drawn considerably aside. Here follow some of my dottings:

A very comfortable kitchen with a

chimney-corner on the south side – immense grate and brilliant fire – large kettle hanging over it by a chain attached to a transverse iron bar – a settle on the left-hand side of the fire – seven fine large men near the fire – two upon the settle, two upon chairs, one in the chimney-corner smoking a pipe, and two standing up – table near the settle with glasses, amongst which is that of myself, who sit nearly in the middle of the room a little way on the right-hand side of the fire.

The floor is of slate; a fine brindled greyhound lies before it on the hearth, and a shepherd's dog wanders about, occasionally going to the door and scratching as if anxious to get out. The company are dressed mostly in the same fashion, brown coats, broad-brimmed hats, and yellowish corduroy breeches with gaiters. One who looks like a labouring man has a white smock and a white hat, patched trousers, and highlows covered with gravel – one has a blue coat.

There is a clock on the right-hand side of the kitchen; a warming-pan hangs close by it on the projecting side of the chimney-corner. On the same side is a large rack containing many plates and dishes of Staffordshire ware. Let me not forget a pair of fire-irons which hang on the right-hand side of the chimney-corner!

I made a great many more dottings, which I shall not insert here. During the whole time I was dotting the most marvellous silence prevailed in the room, broken only by the occasional scratching of the dog against the inside of the door, the ticking of the clock, and the ruttling of the smoker's pipe in the chimney-corner. After I had dotted to my heart's content I closed my book, put the pencil into the loops, then the book into my pocket, drank what remained of my ale, got up, and, after another look at the apartment and its furniture and a leer at the company, departed from the house without ceremony, having paid for the ale when I received it. After walking some fifty yards down the street I turned half round and beheld, as I knew I should, the whole company at the door staring after me. I leered sideways at them for about half a minute, but they stood my leer stoutly. Suddenly I was inspired by a thought. Turning round I confronted them, and pulling my note-book out of my pocket, and seizing my pencil, I fell to dotting vigorously. That was too much for them. As if struck by a panic, my quondam friends turned round and bolted into the house; the rustic-looking man with the smock-frock and gravelled highlows nearly falling down in his eagerness to get in.

The name of the place where this adventure occurred was Cemmaes.

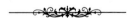

'Outside the Alehouse Door' by George Morland (1763-1804); oils. (*The Tate Gallery, London*)

Gamekeepers' repast. The dead birds appear to be herons, shot, presumably, to preserve fish stocks. From *Grundy's English Views*, c 1857. (*Radio Times Hulton Picture Library*)

A Modern Poacher

Some made poaching their sole occupation, others, poverty stricken, became poachers from necessity. One, at least, was a *born* poacher, as we read in this article from *Country Life* **dated 2 May 1868**

IN the *Cornhill Magazine*, some time since, we were informed in a very interesting article that:

the poacher of the old school, if he ever existed, with his Allan-a-Dale swagger and Robin Hood-like generosity, is as extinct as Dick Turpin. To him has succeeded the poacher of the iron age; member of a ruffianly gang, whose business it is to fill the dealers' shops in town and country, and to get drunk on the proceeds. These gangs vary in numbers and daring, from the top-sawyers of London down to the provincial artists, who are shoemakers or rat-catchers by day, and poachers only by night. The cream of the profession, we fancy, sully not their hands by any meaner occupation, not at least in the day of their glory, 'in the season of the year'. These men, making some large village or town in a good game country or perhaps London itself their head-quarters, carry on operations in a systematic and wholesome fashion. They have their spies and underlings in the neighbourhood of all the large preserves, from whom they receive accurate information as to the quantity of game, the likeliest covers, the move-ments of the keepers, and the character of the local police. In fact, their precautions and their organisation are exactly the same as those of any regular gang of housebreakers.

This is no doubt true generally and to a very great extent, but that there are many of the old order of poachers left is not to be denied. I know of one, at least, who may be so denominated, and he is a poacher *pur et simple*, a poacher not from necessity, nor exactly from taste, but for sheer 'devilment', and he shall stand for a sample of a large family.

This gentleman, who for the sake of euphony and identification we will call Bob Ward, may be said to have been born a poacher.

From earliest infancy he had been initiated into the mysteries of 'ginning', wiring, and netting, and had drank in particulars of many a midnight raid upon the game of his native home almost with his mother's milk. It was his glory to emulate the example of his father, who had been a poacher before him, and to walk in the same opposition to the game laws which his worthy progenitor had set before him.

And let it not be supposed that Bob,

while committing every sort of depredation upon the pheasants and hares of other people and appropriating them for his own use and behoof, would for a moment admit that he was doing any sort of wrong to his neighbour. He regarded all such animals as *ferae naturae*, and, therefore, the property of every man who chose to shoot them. Nothing could convince him of the fallacy of this conviction, and he persisted in maintaining it through evil and good report – with a very small amount of the latter as may be supposed – until age prevented him from showing much active manifestation of its power. It is perhaps a little singular, to say the least of it, that if the appropriation of other people's property was a strictly honest proceeding, the necessity of conducting operations to that end stealthily and in defiance of constituted authority, did not strike him as being somewhat extraordinary, and not exactly in accordance with the usual characteristics of an honest man.

But the fact is, Bob had but an indifferently bad set of advisers from the first; these consisting for the most part of sporting 'gents' and objectionable young farmers who imagined themselves 'up to a thing or two'. Pugilism almost as a matter of course, presented itself to the restless ambition of Mr Ward, and, had that noble science not been unfortunately on the wane, there is no saying, so sterling was his courage, to what heights of glory he might not have soared. The very name of Ward had a pugilistic smack about it, and it was easy by a little genealogical sleight of hand to trace a direct line of relationship from the original 'Jem', the 'Black Diamond' of a former day. The consequence of this pugilistic tendency was many a 'turn-up for a purse', and other amusements of a like exalting character, in which Bob was generally a conspicuous performer. In one of these encounters, in which, however, he fought until his antagonist completely blinded him, and compelled him 'to adopt the early closing movement', as the Corinthians have it, he had the misfortune to be 'bested'. Bob, although exhibiting the most undoubted pluck, and 'taking his gruel like a man', did not give promise of attaining to that finish so necessary to a successful career in the profession.

Poaching appeared specially marked out for him after this. Respectability had not marked him for her own; and Bob started with a grievance, and made war against society and its prescribed rules. No doubt, had he lived nearer the metropolis he would have joined the Reform League, or something of that sort; as it was, he became one of the most determined, systematic, and conscientious poachers of his day and generation.

Too lazy or too independent to work, he lived on in tolerably comfortable circumstances, in open and daring infraction of the Game Laws, and, strange to say, in the enjoyment of considerable popularity among the villagers. For Bob was generous to a fault, and a walking exemplification of the proverb, 'Light come, light go.' Widows and orphans never wanted while Bob was in funds, and there were only too many who were disposed to wink at his delinquencies when they could always claim a share of the plunder without incurring any of the danger. The headkeeper of the neighbouring preserves, which belonged to a nobleman, was a very unpopular man, and delighted in the nickname of 'Gips',

'Poachers Apprehended' by Henry Alken (1785-1851); colour print.
(*Radio Times Hulton Picture Library*)

probably from his Creole-looking face.

Bob's pugilistic peculiarities were not without effect upon the keepers, who entertained a most profound respect for his daring; and there is reason to believe were discreetly absent on many an occasion when it was whispered that Bob and his companions were pursuing their avocations. He made no secret whatever of his intended excursions, and had openly stated his determination to 'do for that Gips', whenever that official should attempt his capture. The keepers, on the other hand, knew what a desperate affair would be any demonstration on their part against Mr Ward's personal liberty, and how 'the nobs' would be 'riled' when they heard of it. Mr Ward, upon the whole, led a very comfortable life, and could supply his patrons with any number of pheasants or hares, either alive or dead, that they might require. His lordship, fearing an affray, offered him a situation as keeper, with a prospect of succession to the chief post, but Bob was deaf to the charmer. Indeed, anything savouring of work and pay was repugnant to his nature. Yet he would have made a splendid keeper, and his knowledge of rearing young pheasants was unequalled.

One night 'Gips' and his men turned out in force, for his lordship had remonstrated concerning the decrease of game, and, if their situations were to be retained, the keepers must put down Bob's gang *vi et armis*. Bob had been heard to say at the 'pub' that some bullets he had were for 'Gips', and that was awkward for him. 'Gips', as headkeeper, carried his gun; all his men were without firearms.

It was terribly dark, and when a shot was fired by the poachers, 'Gips' blazed away at the flash, and managed to capture one of the gang, whom he handcuffed round a tree until the morning. Meanwhile a shot was heard some way off, and the underkeeper was discovered shortly afterwards lying dead in a pool of blood. Bob's hat was found near the spot, and he 'skedaddled' from the country that very hour. The captured poacher was transported for life, having been blinded of an eye. Bob returned after an absence of three or four years, and pursued his avocations on the old domain, without let or hindrance; and even now turns out for a little diversion in the very same preserve where he was so prominent a participator in that dark night's darker deed.

The Reed Harvest

BY T. F. GOODALL

This is an extract from the book entitled *Life and Landscape on the Norfolk Broads* **(1886), produced jointly by P. H. Emerson, the eminent pioneer-photographer, and T. F. Goodall**

BY far the most valuable product of the swamps and rough marshes adjacent to the Broads, is the crop cut yearly from the reedbeds which form so prominent and picturesque a feature in the landscape. The dense green masses of this plant, so characteristic of the Broads in the summertime, after putting forth their purple flower tassels, and undergoing the most beautiful changes of subtle and delicate colour in the autumn, shed their leaves, and by Christmas nothing remains but the tall, slender, sapless stems with the withered flowers at the tips.

The cutting and harvesting of the reed afford profitable employment to the Broadman, marshman, or farmhand during the winter months, when other work is scarce; and whenever the weather permits they may be seen busily plying the meak amid the tall yellow masses, or bringing the loaded marshboat across the Broad. Each of these four plates portrays some characteristic incident of this picturesque labour. First is the single figure of a reed cutter at work. Standing with his crotch-boots in the water, he bends over in the act of cutting a fresh shoof, those just cut lying behind him bound with a band of a few crossed and twisted reeds. The shoof is the unit of reed measurement, and the size of it is gauged by the cutter by placing his two thumbs together on the bundle, and spreading the hands wide. Then he turns one hand without shifting the position of the tip of the little finger, which forms the pivot; and if the thumb of that hand just reaches the little finger of the other, the shoof is of the right dimension, or three spans in circumference. Reed is sold by the fathom: six shooves make a fathom, and six score fathoms go to the hundred, for cutting which the sum of thirty shillings is paid by the reed farmer in wages; so that the men get just one halfpenny for each bundle they cut and tie. The sum a man can earn in a day depends very much on the thickness of the crop. In a good bed, where the reed grows very close together, he can earn four shillings by a good day's work; but in some places it is so thin and scattered that he may not be able to make more than one. Being a piece-worker, the reed cutter is his own master, and consequently the work is much in demand by those

A reed-cutter at work in the 1880s.
(*The British Library, London*)

men – often some of the best hands – who like, occasionally, to relieve the monotony of existence by a prolonged drinking-bout, or to whom the attractions of a coursing meeting on the marshes, or a shooting match, are irresistible. When cut, the shooves are stood on end, leaning against each other in stacks on the bank of the nearest dyke, till the marshboat conveys them to the staithe, where they are ricked.

'Towing reed' illustrates the usual method of getting the loaded boat along the narrow water-arteries which intersect the marshes, and afford communication with the reedbeds. Sturdy of frame and strong-featured, a fine type of the Norfolk peasant is this tower. Then we have the men at the rick on the staithe, at the head of a long dyke stretching far away to the distance, and again a gang of workers forming a busy scene in the heart of the reed grounds.

The reed harvest does not commence till close on Christmas, when the sap is thoroughly dried from the stems, and must be discontinued as soon as the young shoots sprout in early April, for then it is impossible to cut the old crop without injury to the new. Thus no more than four months at the most are available, and in bad winters much of the reedbed remains uncut, for work has to be suspended when the water is too high, or when the roots of the plants are clogged with ice and frozen snow. When a prolonged frost occurs, much of the reed is of necessity left standing, but it is not wasted, as it remains, without serious deterioration, till the next winter, and so forms a double crop. Where the growth is very thin, and one year's produce would scarcely pay for cutting, and also when the reed merchants have large stocks accumulated, and the demand is not very brisk, the reed is purposely left standing till the following year. For storing shooves are placed so as to form a sloping thatch: surplus stocks can thus be kept dry, and in good marketable condition, for years.

The water-marshes are generally farmed by the dealer in reed and 'shoof-stuff' or litter, who pays from ten to twelve shillings rent per acre for the right to cut the produce of all kinds, including fagots from the alder-bushes. His chief customers for the reed are the builders and thatchers, and the price obtained varies from £5 to £6 for the hundred fathoms, according to the length of the stems. What is called 'short reed' is

Ricking the reed. (*The British Library, London*)

about six feet in length; this is used for thatching the roofs of farm buildings and dwelling houses, and, if laid and fastened in a workmanlike fashion, is very durable. A reed thatch, of proper thickness, will remain impervious to the weather for fifty years, or if the pitch of the roof be steep, so that the water has no chance to lie upon it, it will last eighty years, and even longer. 'Long-reed' – the best shooves of which will measure nine feet in height – is used extensively by builders for the party walls of dwellings and for the ceilings of rooms, being nailed between laths and the floor-joists for the latter, and between battens for the former purpose. The round stems and intervening crevices of the reeds afford a surface admirably adapted to holding plaster, which clings to it tenaciously, obtaining a better grip than is afforded by laths, and never cracks or falls. Imbedded in plaster, and sealed from the air, there is no end to the durability of reed: in dwellings which have been demolished after an existence of three centuries, the reed has been found intact and sound as when it left the rick.

Starlings are the chief enemies of the reed farmer. During November and December the beds must be well watched of an evening, or the myriads of these birds will do irreparable damage, for then the starlings congregate in immense hosts, which darken the sky, circling and wheeling round the marshes. They will,

During the reed harvest. *(The British Library, London)*

unless driven off with guns, alight on the reed stalks and beat them down to a flat surface, on which they settle and pitch camp for the night. Many pounds' worth of reed is annually destroyed by these pests, much of the best and thickest of the crop being so broken and flattened by their combined charges that it is completely spoiled and wasted.

Many kinds of birds find a shelter among the reed during the breeding season. Wild duck and water-hen, coot and teal, educate their fluffy broods in deep seclusion among the roots and on the little pools around which they grow. In the tall stems the reed-bird builds its little nest, some three or four feet from the ground, neatly woven, and attached to five or six of the stalks, drawn together with threads of tough grass, which securely support the structure where the young birds are hatched from the tiny eggs, and rocked to and fro by the breeze. The men, when cutting, come across many of these nests, still in sound condition, and so firmly fastened to the reeds that they hold together when severed at the roots. A lively little bird is the reed-sparrow, fond of late hours and loud songs: far from shy, this nightingale of the marshes delights in a disturbance, and if a stone be pitched into the bush where he is sitting, he acknowledges the intrusion by a burst of melody.

Notwithstanding laws to the contrary, nest-robbing is still a very common

Towing the reed. (*The British Library, London*)

practice, and is more destructive to wild-fowl than all the guns. The egg of the plover has always been in great demand as a delicacy for the table of the gourmet. We have heard of an old marshman who reproved a sportsman for shooting a plover in the winter, because the bird to his mind represented so many eggs in the summer: from his point of view the bird should be protected for the sake of the eggs. Besides the plovers' eggs which are taken and openly marketed, large numbers of the nests of birds, more or less rare, are harried on the marshes, the eggs being often procured for secret sale to customers who from their position should be among the first to discourage such proceedings. This, and the senseless slaughter of very rare birds, because they are rare, has led to the practical annihilation of several species which used to be fairly common on the wild wastes and swampy marshes. The boom of the bittern is no longer a familiar sound; when heard at all, it is immediately silenced by a charge of shot. The feathered stranger finds no hospitality, and when exceptionally rare or distinguished, even the breeding season is not respected: indeed to many birds it is the most fatal season, for then they are resplendent in their courting costume, and especially sought after by those whose taste for decoration is completely satisfied by a glass case of stuffed plumage.

Winter

BY DENIS CURLING (1921-42)

An icy wind rustles the fallen leaves;
Bare trees grope skywards like a clutching hand;
A robin flutters in the eaves
Above the window where old Winter weaves
The frosty patterns of his frozen land.

A muffled man hurries along the lane,
His nose aglow, rubbing his smarting eyes;
He passes, and is gone again;
Only the great gaunt trees remain
Pale in the starlight from the cruel skies.

Old Winter with his flowing beard and hair,
A young and carefree child not long ago.
Played in the sunny meadows where
The grass is frosty now and trees stand bare
In twilight leaden with the coming snow.

'Frosty Morning' (1813) by J. M. W. Turner (1775-1851); oils. To the title Turner added a quotation from James Thomson, the Scottish poet: 'The rigid hoar frost melts before his beams'. The picture shows a sunny day in winter; hedgers and ditchers are starting work in the fields. (*The Tate Gallery, London. Photograph: John Webb*)

The Lonely Birdscarer

BY W. H. HUDSON (1841-1922)

Published in 1910, *A Shepherd's Life* is the source of the following anecdote. The location is the open bleakness of Salisbury Plain

IT was in March, bitterly cold, with an east wind which had been blowing many days, and overhead the sky was of a hard, steely grey. I was cycling along the valley of the Ebble, and finally leaving it pushed up a long steep slope and set off over the high plain by a dusty road with the wind hard against me. A more desolate scene than the one before me it would be hard to imagine, for the land was all ploughed and stretched away before me, an endless succession of vast grey fields, divided by wire fences. On all that space there was but one living thing in sight, a human form, a boy, far away on the left side, standing in the middle of a big field with something which looked like a gun in his hand. Immediately after I saw him he, too, appeared to have caught sight of me, for turning he set off running as fast as he could over the ploughed ground towards the road, as if intending to speak to me. The distance he would have to run was about a quarter of a mile and I doubted that he would be there in time to catch me, but he ran fast and the wind was against me, and he arrived at the road just as I got to that point. There by the side of the fence he stood, panting from his race, his handsome face glowing with colour, a boy about twelve or thirteen, with a fine strong figure, remarkably well dressed for a bird-scarer. For that was what he was, and he carried a queer, heavy-looking old gun. I got off my wheel and waited for him to speak, but he was silent, and continued regarding me with the smiling countenance of one well pleased with himself. 'Well?' I said, but there was no answer; he only kept on smiling.

'What did you want?' I demanded impatiently.

'I didn't want anything.'

'But you started running here as fast as you could the moment you caught sight of me.'

'Yes, I did.'

'Well, what did you do it for – what was your object in running here?'

The Crow-Boy's Christmas Lunch by 'Phiz' (Hablot Knight Browne, 1815-82), from the *Illustrated London News*, 21 December 1850. (*The Fotomas Index*)

'Just to see you pass,' he answered.

It was a little ridiculous and vexed me at first, but by and by when I left him, after some more conversation, I felt rather pleased; for it was a new and somewhat flattering experience to have any person run a long distance over a ploughed field, burdened with a heavy gun, 'just to see me pass'.

But it was not strange in the circumstances; his hours in that grey, windy desolation must have seemed like days, and it was a break in the monotony, a little joyful excitement in getting to the road in time to see a passer-by more closely, and for a few moments gave him a sense of human companionship. I began even to feel a little sorry for him, alone there in his high, dreary world, but presently thought he was better off and better employed than most of his fellows poring over miserable books in school, and I wished we had a more rational system of education for the agricultural districts, one which would not keep the children shut up in a room during all the best hours of the day, when to be out of doors, seeing, hearing, and doing, would fit them so much better for the life-work before them.

Trees in Winter

FROM *UNDER THE GREENWOOD TREE*, 1872 BY THOMAS HARDY (1840-1928)

TO dwellers in a wood almost every species of tree has its voice as well as its feature. At the passing of the breeze the fir-trees sob and moan no less distinctly than they rock; the ash hisses amid its quiverings; the beech rustles while its flat boughs rise and fall. And winter, which modifies the note of such trees as shed their leaves, does not destroy its individuality. On a cold and starry Christmas Eve within living memory, a man was passing up a lane near Mellstock Cross, in the darkness of a plantation that whispered thus distinctively to his intelligence ... and to his eyes, casually glancing upward, the silver and black-stemmed birches with their characteristic tufts, the pale grey boughs of beech, the dark-creviced elm, all appeared now as black and flat outlines upon the sky, wherein the white stars twinkled so vehemently that their flickering seemed like the flapping of wings.

A Birket Foster illustration from *Birds, Bees and Blossoms* of 1858.
(*The British Library, London*)

ℒetter XXVII

BY GILBERT WHITE (1720-93)

For twenty years Gilbert White, a country parson, wrote a series of letters to Thomas Pennant and Daines Barrington containing his observations on wild life. It was Barrington who suggested publication, in 1770, but it was not until eighteen years later that White perpared anything for the press, and the book appeared in 1789

TO THOMAS PENNANT, ESQUIRE

Selborne, 22 February 1770.

Dear Sir,

Hedgehogs abound in my gardens and fields. The manner in which they eat their roots of the plantain in my grass-walks is very curious: with their upper mandible, which is much longer than their lower, they bore under the plant, and so eat the root off upwards, leaving the tuft of leaves untouched. In this respect they are serviceable, as they destroy a very troublesome weed; but they deface the walks in some measure by digging little round holes. It appears, by the dung that they drop upon the turf, that beetles are no inconsiderable part of their food. In June last I procured a litter of four or five young hedgehogs, which appeared to be about five or six days old; they, I find, like puppies, are born blind, and could not see when they came to my hands. No doubt their spines are soft and flexible at the time of their birth, or else the poor dam would have but a bad time of it in the critical moment of parturition: but it is plain that they soon harden; for these little pigs had such stiff prickles on their backs and sides as would easily have fetched blood, had they not been handled with caution. Their spines are quite white at this age; and they have little hanging ears, which I do not remember to be discernible in the old ones. They can, in part, at this age draw their skin down over their faces; but are not able to contract themselves into a ball as they do, for the sake of defence, when full grown. The reason, I suppose, is because the curious muscle that enables the creature to roll itself up into a ball was not then arrived at its full tone and firmness. Hedgehogs make a deep and warm *hybernaculum* with leaves and moss, in which they conceal themselves for the winter: but I never could find that they stored in any winter provision, as some quadrupeds certainly do.

I have discovered an anecdote with respect to the fieldfare (*turdus pilaris*), which I think is particular enough: this bird, though it sits on trees in the daytime, and procures the greatest part of its food from whitethorn hedges; yea, moreover, builds on very high trees; as may be seen by the *fauna suecica;* yet always appears with us to roost on the ground. They are seen to come in flocks just before it is dark, and to settle and nestle among the heath on our forest. And besides, the larkers, in dragging their nets by night, frequently catch them in the wheat-stubbles; while the bat-fowlers, who take many redwings in the hedges, never entangle any of this species. Why these birds, in the matter of roosting, should differ from all their congeners, and from themselves also with respect to their proceedings by day, is a fact for which I am by no means able to account.

I have somewhat to inform you of concerning the moose-deer; but in general foreign animals fall seldom in my way; my little intelligence is confined to the narrow sphere of my own observations at home.

The British Library, London

'February in the Isle of Wight' (1866) by John Brett (1830-1902); watercolour plus body colour; detail. (*Birmingham Museum and Art Gallery*)

Morning Showers

BY JOHN CLARE (1793-1864)

Now the meadow water smokes,
And the hedgerow's dripping oaks
Pitter-patter all around
And dimple the once-dusty ground;
The spinners' threads about the weeds
Are hung with little drops in beads;
Clover silver-green becomes,
And purple-blue surrounds the plums,
And every place breathes fresh and fair
When morning pays her visit there.

The waterfowl with suthering wing
Dive down the river, splash and spring
Up to the very clouds again
That sprinkle scuds of coming rain,
That fly and drizzle all the day
Till dripping grass is turned to grey;
The various clouds [now] move or lie
Like mighty travellers in the sky,
All mountainous and ridged and curled,
That may have travelled round the world.
When the rain at midday stops,
Spandles glitter in the drops,
And, as each thread a sunbeam was,
Cobwebs glitter in the grass.
The sheep all loaded with the rain
Try to shake it off again,
And ere dried by wind and sun
The load will scarcely let them run.

Song of the Barrow

BY ANTHONY C. WEST (born 1910)

Described as 'the doyen of Ulster fiction-writers', Anthony West has hitherto achieved greater renown in the USA than at home. This short story is highly evocative of the Irish countryside, and of its people

AS perhaps a beast may hear, over many years the sound was for me a pure percept unconnected with any concept or idea; it was always sad but not ominous. The first time I heard it I was a child on the hazy edge of sense. It came from the coal-house door that had sagged on its hinges and scraped an edge on the concrete floor; then infrequently a breeze might make it by rubbing two branches together, and usually the weathercock above the high ceiling in my bedroom when in the night the wind would veer or back from calm to the wet south-west and coming storm.

It is with me yet, two-thirds of my life lived, and now naturally laden with all that memory may endow – an almost archetypal sound, though still uncaught and ephemeral.

I know that springs come and go, the earth opening to the sun like a flower and then dying again; that the seasons pass inevitably, springtime unto harvest; and ultimately I know I will hear sound for the last time.

May brought life and activity to the peat bogs. In their own right these lake-side bogs were aloof, exciting places, more dead than lifeless rock and yet somehow beyond death; but I never more than half trusted them – they had too many facile moods, even for May, and sometimes they were dour solemn still-silent places where autumn seemed always to lurk in the dense bracken: the mereing lake-water deep and peat-stained and ominous, the strands foot-sucking and quaking like a disturbing dream.

When turf-time came I prayed through the dull school week for Saturday's weather to be fine, and when the free day came I would rise early and to avoid chores slip away softly across the pasture fields, through the templed beech wood, down the steep hill flank to the first lake; then I could look down on the busy heat-shimmering waste that was the great Rivary Bog, its husbandmen no larger than mice.

One early Saturday I came to Rivary, counting more than a hundred men and boys at work. Some were cutting out, some making mud-turf and shaping the thick-spread glar into loaves with their hands, standing shin-deep in the mud.

This craft of peat-getting was quite

familiar to me, had I not mind-known it I would have remembered by blood and bone, each rhythmic gesture an ancient ritual act of kinship to the earth. Half-dazed with content I watched the age-old movements – cut, sling, catch; cut, sling, catch – each block of moist blood-dark humus no larger nor smaller than another.

The forenoon almost spent, finally I attached myself to a man I knew, who worked a peat bank with his son's help. The son stood above with wide-fingered open hands, letting the slippery bricks of earth drop easily to rest within them as though he were catching eggs, for when wet the turves were fragile as eggs.

Layer by layer, step by neat step like the unbuilding of a wall the old man worked methodically down the face of the peat seam. It was warm and airless in the hole, and a patch of sweat stuck the shirt to his back. He was a big, powerful, raw-boned man with thonged, weather-beaten, age-mottled forearms – an aged man for such a young son. I knew there were seven girls in the family and only this, the youngest, a boy who favoured his mother in the face but had his father's high strong Norman nose and big-boned frame.

He was a cocksure youth, which was natural enough with eight adoring women in his home, but he was also pleasant and seriously responsible, conscious of heritage to farm and name. He joked with me as he passed to and fro with his sideless barrow, with one quick tip sliding the turves onto their ends on the heather-stripped spongy sward so they could dry out and drain enough to hold together for windrowing.

And often, guilelessly, he endeavoured to impress me that manhood was securely with him and that the four years in his eighteen made him full adult and tied me to boyhood. He walked with arrogance, aware of his broad back and deep chest cage, square wrists and bulging fore-arms; handling with extravagant ease the heavy barrow, its solid wooden wheel on wooden axle nostalgically ululant, the dolorous sounds taking sides in my mind with a waft of cloud-darkened wind that moved over rush and reed and arced the bees' itinerant flight. I shuddered, anxious with the feeling my mother said was caused by a goose walking over the place my grave would be and making me see always a grey goose with wet, pink-webbed, cold feet.

But a golden swath of sunlight came again, and hands behind head, lying on the warm earth with half-shut eyes I watched him, his fair freckled skin sun-red down to the collar-bones and fading to girlish whiteness on his hairless chest; the back of his strong neck a darker red, the rim of light fair hair tonsured by the cap-band and made dark with sweat. Like a gage he wore in his cap a sprig of elder, against the early flies that annoyed him when he had both hands on the barrow handles.

Without envy I gloried in his energy, thinking it wonderful to be so strong and capable, so tireless and lightly moving; to be so unerring in the catching of the upspinning peat and so craft-concious in gesture, hand, timing, and body; to be so free, so close to manhood, his coming and going no longer questioned and his word accepted. Packy was his name – Packy Reilly.

And he became for me a sudden symbol for the May and all of spring's fulfilment; a concrete being but a fit omen for the time; and I was proud of

167

nim as I knew the father was proud, and because so obviously did the old man love him, so also did I love him and loved the father for loving so.

By midday the communal fires were kindled and when the water boiled the cooks called. For me the meal was a rural Eucharist. I ate with their eating and filled myself with their satisfaction. They were all hungry and tired, some of them not having tasted food since dawn, for many came to the bog from afar. Before the bread's breaking each one removed his headgear, the older men doing so with embarrassment and rubbing hopeful hands on naked domes, still not convinced after so many years that their hairs had gone for good.

The Reillys shared their food with me. I knew beforehand their butter was sweet and not rancid. In return I would help Packy windrow, a stooping task the old man did not relish. The open fires gleamed genially, the flames making fairy whirlpools of hot air that swayed the hazel canopy overhead. Replete, the men lolled back and smoked, talking of other bog days with slow memories that might have been their own or those of past ancestors. I larked with the younger lads for half an hour, jumping bog-holes and battling with turf-sods.

In the hills' lee the flat of marsh and bog was hot as August and after the windrowing I walked carefully to the lake's edge to bathe and saw the darkness delve down fifteen feet to a weed-green bottom, a sublacustrine world of eel, salmon, perch, bream, and insensate pike; airless, aloof, and somehow more frightening than the grey rock-rimmed restless depths of the sea-loch. And again, unreasonably, I heard the peat barrow's nocturnal wheel song, two lugubrious notes it had, like the ass just then braying; a little minor chord, maybe B-flat and E. It moved across the bog; two score other barrows sobbed similarly and a hawk-like cuckoo made the swallows give their low two-noted warning that was the same tone as the barrow song; all sounds flowing softly down into this little hollow of music.

But I gazed about, satisfying myself that May was still safe and sound in sun, wind and cloud. And then I first saw the bream. I thought a hand of wind was fingering the oil-calm surface but then I saw the dorsal fins slicing the water. This was the first bream school I had ever seen, this little mad miracle of countless sperming fish troubling the water. I crouched staring, knowing normally they were shy and secretive bottom feeders and now bold and careless in their seething shoal. They bore inward till I could see their forms and distorted shadows in the sunlit shallows: large and small – some of the big ones twenty pounds. I wanted to keep them to myself but I also wanted to catch them and could not catch them all. Turning to the bog I shouted, cupping the call with both hands and throwing it aloft like stone from sling.

'Bream! Bream! A school – a school!'

I might have sworn ransom to the first who reached me. Every man and boy downed work and doubled over, falling, swearing, laughing in their haste and splashing into the water beside me with staring eyes and open mouths and chests heaving with the race. I got out of the way, for they scared me a little, reminding me of tales I had read somewhere about mobs trampling living bodies underfoot.

Excitement owned them all; uncaring, they plunged after the bream, slashing

168

'Mountainous Landscape. Afterglow' attributed to John Varley (1778-1842).
(*Victoria and Albert Museum, London; Crown copyright*)

with sticks, sleans, and forks; falling over each other, inadvertently hitting and hurting each other so several petty scrimmages arose, as if they were also drunk with life and May and obeyed a race law in primitive abandon, the rut-drowsed fish quite lost in the splashing.

Packy Reilly was in the van, the first to catch a big one with his bare hands, kneeling belly-deep in water and holding up the curving life-arc in unconscious Protean mime. Now and again a big flat brown form rose through the air and bounced on the grass, pitched quivering off fork prongs or half stunned with sticks. Soon two score and more fish flapped on the grass, slapping against each other, enduring agony, their element but a few tragic feet away.

Slowly the wild enthusiasm died down as belatedly the bream reacted to danger and moved out into deep water. One by one the exhausted humans waded ashore, now slightly self-conscious in proportion to their years. They started stripping and wringing out their clothes.

'Packy! Where's Packy?' a strong imperious voice demanded. 'Packy!'

Talk, laughter, and all movement froze save for the slip-slap of the dying bream. All heads turned to old Reilly, then to each other wonderingly as if they'd been asked an awkward question. They looked about, over the grass by their feet, behind each other as though big Packy were a hop-o'-my-thumb and crouching at an instep; but they never lifted an eye to the lake.

'Packy! Where is he?' Reilly roared, his staring eyes wide-shot with fear. He caught a neighbour's arm and bellowed Packy in his ear as if the man were hiding the youth for a poor joke. Then he listened to the stark silence through which tripped faintly off the scrubland the name and came light-somely, gaily back – Packy! Packy! Packy! – answering itself each time with many voices more faintly, faintly, faint until it also wearied of the search and fell silent; but not for me. The name Packy had leagued with the barrow's two-noted song.

They all wasted seconds to arrive perforce at the same frightening conclusion; not so much wasted as ill spent the time in case there might have been a happier answer. Every eye now moved reluctantly to the mud-stirred lake and I saw again the dull depth-fall to the green bottom that could have as many feet again of liquid mud under the weeds.

With a startling animal howl Reilly ran into the water. He forced his thighs against the increasing pressure with grotesque high prancing: falling flat, disappearing, rising, surging on, his shirt now flimsy and clinging to his frame as the sweat had stuck a patch of it to him in the bog-hole. As a lash his wailing seared me with new guiltiness, for his cries had the same pitch and cadence as the barrow's dirge and the ass's bray, and Reilly now choired requiem for Packy and also for my May.

Two neighbours ran after him, catching his arms, talking and trying to restrain him. They knew he could not swim.

'Let me out!' he mouthed. 'Lemme go, God damn ye, lemme go!'

He struggled, all friends now enemies, spraying the water into a rainbow . . . 'I'll kill ye if ye don't let go of me! Packy . . .' The two men closed in and he gave up, sobbing and so spent that they had to half lift him back as if he had just been rescued.

Three other men, strong swimmers,

had stripped and gone into deep water. Their black heads bobbing like otters at play, they dived together, round white backsides turning up as they disappeared, and then again and again the black heads bobbed, gasping and spewing, taking fresh breaths and going down again. One man waded in exhausted, saying something about being caught in the bottom weeds and all heads nodded wisely with knowing ayes of assent droning like an amen. The man was vomiting noisily, his ridged rippling stomach going flat and hollow with each painful retch.

The other two persisted, coming up, going down – black heads, white bodies, bubbles and writhing water that still seemed harmless under the sun. Then one surfaced and made signs to the shore with his right hand. Voices said: 'They've got him!' A boy who knew no better cheered and someone clouted him. He fell head over heels and began to snuffle and another lad sniggered. I wanted to laugh as well, although I knew laughter would now be weeping.

Old Reilly paid no heed and sat whimpering on a stone, muttering now not his son's name but the name of his wife over and over again: Bridie, Bridie, Bridie . . . as though asking her for comfort while attempting to make up a reasonable story, his craggy peat-stained hands fumbling over his shining bald head – doubtfully, as though he had already disremembered what he had been starting to say to his wife and did not know how to set about rethinking it.

His grief disturbed everyone. They glanced at him shyly – ashamed and scared of him and his sorrow, and wishing he would take it somewhere else. They were fully sympathetic but quite unable to measure or match with approximate agony the agony of his wild suffering. They all knew as I knew that Packy was his only son and last one, the mother no longer fit to bear again. And as dogs will sometimes rend a howling injured companion, the old man's remote despair and the distant grumbling mystery of it angered them and made them impersonally hate him.

I knew none of them could think clearly above the storm of the mourning; they were not hard men but none was subtle; it filled their heads like shells' sea-sound, muting the near and stately tread of death. Nervously the fathers sought for sons with their eyes and gratefully named them in health.

The divers had gone down together, staying down a long time, the witnesses holding their breaths as well and only exhaling when the men broke surface and turned to the shore, one stroking with his left arm and the other stroking with his right, their right and left hands towing something heavy.

All the spectators made cross-signs, glancing furtively at the father in case he noticed their premature fatalism. For the heavy thing between the swimmers offended them all and I sensed they would as soon have left it there in the weeds under water. One older man went quietly to Reilly, bending down privately to whisper the news; but he was not heeded nor heard at all and Reilly's sorrow-surly indifference to Packy's reappearance seemed to concede victory to death.

The divers had dragged Packy into shallow water, the boy coming in face down, his head hanging between hunched shoulders. They gladly gave him up to the dozen men who met them.

A hundred yards out the bream school

One of a series of six coloured prints showing flax production in Ireland, drawn and engraved by
W. Hincks, and published in 1791. This one shows a 'View taken near Scarva in the County of
Downe representing Ploughing, Sowing the Flax Seed and Harrowing'.
(*By courtesy of the Victoria and Albert Museum, London. Photograph: Brian Hunt; John R. Freeman
& Co*)

still milled about, death-indifferent in life-lust. My mind turned over everything again: Packy, May's prototype and now like the stranded fish; the fish chastely life-lusting to their own increase with palid sperm sinking greyly unto myriad cold eggs that would hatch under the sun's breast and make more fish for other Mays. I glanced nervously at the clump of men and boys, all of them male and hard-lined like myself, muscled and set and manned to beget and suddenly I saw not males but females gentle-breasted and watching Packy's form with anxious eyes, wise in their sorrow.

I shuddered and looked for relief over the fields, lakes, hills, and distant mountains anchored in the sea ... I could only peer at Packy from the corner of an eye, ashamed to stare openly, the youth now a stranger and something quite secret and personal.

Instead, I watched the two weary divers and their lean living bodies, their red necks and forearms as Packy's neck and forearms had been sun-red. One of them held his nose in forefinger and thumb and cleared his ears, then blew through each nostril with small tearing sounds. The second man copied and both started to jog up and down to keep warm. Old Reilly moaned and swayed on his stone.

Packy had been laid face down on a round boulder and two men were pumping his arms, a third astride his buttocks and rising up the ribs with his hands much as hands were held, thumb to thumb, when shaping the magma of mud-turf.

The wet pants and shirt cockled wryly on the body, the taut proud muscles now lax and flabby ... I could hardly understand. I had seen death coming to animals but there had always been blood; now there was no blood – just pale loose laxity. And I was disturbed because the abandoned lying of the form to the earth made me see little difference between earth and form, the blond hair now dank beaver-brown with young green water-weeds in it and a garland gage of weeds wound round his waist.

The sobbing father paid no heed and the men kept working on Packy. The men round the body looked at each other and shrugged, and one by one the observers removed their headgear and the old men still ran tentative hands over their bald domes: this not for the bread's breaking.

No one noticed my departure and that it was unseen seemed ominously condemning. I stepped over the dying still-living fish that smelled faintly of lake mud, their gills hopelessly gnawing the cruel air.

Looking back, I saw the knot of men and boys, resembling flies gathered on a mirror against the lake-caught sun. By the roads, I told myself. I will go home slowly this day by the roads and maybe find a man or woman or young fair girl going my way and we will talk and walk together and listen to each other's livingness.

A wild duck startled me. Absently I stopped to count the blue-washed eggs thinking that if there were ten Packy was dead but if eleven he was alive. There were eight eggs as the bird flew swift and low to the lake, banking across the mourners and glancing over the scrub-land like a bullet. I knew she would faithfully orbit her nest until I went away.

Distance knitted now and the bog men seemed to merge into one small motion-less figure by the strand. Two martins with very white vests came together overhead: turning as one, then treading the air and coming beak to beak, chuckling to each other at the mallard's foolishness and fear.

This world of nature was once my whole world and demi-paradise; no other angel present save the kindly ones that graced me to live peacefully with any beauty eye could discover; no sickness, sorrow, nor affliction, no suffering nor death; all humans no more than young and old and only incidentally male and female by shape and member as animals were male and female.

A bird might fall through age or accident, hawks took their due toll, foxes seized weakling lambs, and gulls and grey crows picked the white bones, stoats lusted after rabbits: but these were all natural departures and deaths, if deaths at all; life thriving at the expense of life with reason and unknown purpose much as leaf-fall fed the next bud-burst: these were the slow eternal things, as the year was and the seasons; one might not waste too much pity on them.

Old people lived stiffly, safely on and babies thrived; and although the parish sexton – that round-backed ancient with grey quiet points for eyes, always with red sub-earthly clay under his long nails – although he often marked with lingering bell a neighbour's passing, he also tolled imperatively for worship, joyously for marriages, and contemplatively for the angelus.

I passed an old elder-bush and pinched off a leafy crown, smelling the sap-sour scent of the wounded stem. Packy's gage had been elder and I examined the plant, feigning interest in it but only to beg time, to delay what I now had to think while not knowing how to think, since I had no concepts ready to fit my feelings in this new territory of my soul. I was only a boy, and yet no man might guide me here save that which for well or for ill was the becoming man in me.

Crushing the fetid leaves in my hand I faced the change at last in its unresolved totality and acknowledged for the first time that my world was also full of people – humans, human-kind – not only inhabited by shadows, fixed institutions, and the elemental movement of wind and star. Tears were running down my cheeks and not all of them for Packy nor for myself nor for my May, but for strange self-loneliness.

Down by the lake two dots that were men led a larger dot that was a horse and cart toward the strand, and I knew this was to be Packy's bier and May's bier and bier also for fourteen feckless years of life that counted infant, child, and boy. And I knew the cortège would wend slowly up the valley, Packy lying on the cart's scratched dusty floor, the unspring ironshod wheels sinking to the naves at times in the ruts cut deeply in the peat and jolting his head and jerking his limbs as if he tossed in sleep; maybe he was still asleep, or reborn, or undying into death as the bream took time to die.

Perhaps the men would think kindly to strew the cart's floor with rush and marsh mint and wild thyme and line the box with asphodel and pearly ropes of hawthorn and set a sprig of elder between the horse's ears to drive away the flies.

And soon now the church bell from its high place would clang across the parish, lifting all heads to hear, between each slow strike, its own long-dying note – the sound of the barrow's trundle-song and the scrape of the coal-house door of my childhood and the first wild world-cracking shriek of an infant.

The Wheelwright's Shop

BY GEORGE STURT (1863-1927)

Coming from a family of Surrey wheelwrights, George Sturt was well qualified to write *The Wheelwright's Shop* **— perhaps his finest book — from which this chapter has been taken**

To say that the business I started into in 1884 was old-fashioned is to understate the case: it was a 'folk' industry, carried on in a 'folk' method. And circumstances made it perhaps more intensely so to me than it need have been. My father might just possibly, though I don't think he would, have shown me more modern aspects of it; but within my first month he took ill of the illness he died of five months later. Consequently I was left to pick up the business as best I could from 'the men'. There were never any 'hands' with us. Eight skilled workmen or apprentices, eight friends of the family, put me up to all they could: and since some of them had been born and trained in little old country shops, while this of my father's was not much better, the lore I got from then was of the country through and through.

The objects of the work too were provincial. There was no looking far afield for customers. Farmers rarely more then five miles away; millers, brewers, a local grocer or builder or timber-merchant or hop-grower – for such and no others did the ancient shop still cater, as it had done for nearly two centuries. And so we got curiously intimate with the peculiar needs of the neighbourhood. In farm-wagon or dung-cart, barley-roller, plough, water-barrel, or what not, the dimensions we chose, the curves we followed (and almost every piece of timber was curved) were imposed upon us by the nature of the soil in this or that farm, the gradient of this or that hill, the temper of this or that customer or his choice perhaps in horseflesh. The carters told us their needs. To satisfy the carter, we gave another half-inch of curve to the wagon-bottom, altered the hooks for harness on the shafts, hung the water-barrel an inch nearer to the horse or an inch farther away, according to requirements.

One important point, which it's true was not always important (for hard roads, for instance) but was sometimes very important indeed, was to make the wheels of wagon or dung-cart 'take the routs', as we said. A variant of this was to get the wheels of a wagon to 'follow', the hind wheels cutting the same ruts as the front. One inch of variation was allowed, no more. The track of new dung-cart or

Wheelwrights at work, around the turn of the century. (*Kodak Museum, Harrow*)

wagon might measure 5 feet 10½ inches or 5 feet 11½ inches 'over', that is, from outside to outside. A miry lane at a farm revealed to me the importance of keeping to this measurement. Two parallel ruts went all down the lane, deep as the hub of a cart-wheel. Many carts, for many years perhaps, had followed there; and plainly the lane would be impassable for any cart or wagon with wheels too wide asunder or too narrow. So, the wheel-spaces were standardised.

This was but one of the endless details the complete wheelwright had to know all about. For the complete wheelwright, acquiring skill of eyes and hands to make a wheel, was good enough workman then for the job of building a wagon through-out and painting it too; and all this was expected of him. There was a tale (of another shop than mine) of an aged man who, having built and painted a wagon, set about 'writing' (lettering) the owner's name and address on the small name-board fixed to the off front side. He managed all right until he came to the address, 'Swafham' or 'Swayle', but this word puzzled him. He scratched his head, at last had to own himself baffled; and appealed to his mate. 'Let's see, Gearge,' he said, 'blest if I ain't forgot how you makes a Sway!'

Gearge showed him.

Truly there were mysteries enough, without the mystery of 'writing', for an unlettered man. Even the mixing and putting on of the paint called for experi-ence. The first two coats, of Venetian-red for the underworks and shafts and 'lid colour' (lead colour) for the 'body', prepared the way for the putty, which couldn't be 'knocked-up' by instinct; and then came the last coat, of red-lead for the wheels and Prussian-blue for the body, to make all look smart and showy.

Not any of this could be left wholly to an apprentice. Apprentices, after a year or two, might be equal to making and painting a wheelbarrow. But it was a painful process with them learning the whole trade. Seven years was thought not too long. After seven years, a young man, newly out of his time was held likely to pick up more of his craft in the next twelve months than he had dreamt of before. By then too he should have won the skill that came from wounds. For it was a saying of my grandfather's that nobody could learn to make a wheel without chopping his knee half a dozen times.

There was nothing for it but practice and experience of every difficulty. Reasoned science for us did not exist. 'Theirs not to reason why.' What we had to do was to live up to the local wisdom of our kind; to follow the customs, and work to the measurements, which had been tested and corrected long before our time in every village shop all across the country. A wheelwright's brain had to fit itself to this by dint of growing into it, just as his back had to fit into the supplenesses needed on the saw-pit, or his hands into the movements that would plane a felloe 'true out o wind'. Science? Our two-foot rules took us no nearer to exactness than the sixteenth of an inch: we used to make or adjust special gauges for the nicer work; but very soon a stage was reached when eye and hand were left to their own cleverness, with no guide to help them. So the work was more of an art – a very fascinating art – than a science; and in this art, as I say, the brain had its share. A good wheelwright knew by art but not by reasoning the proportion to keep between spokes and felloes; and so too a good smith knew how  tight a two-and-a-half-inch tyre should be made for a five-foot wheel and how tight for a four-foot, and so on. He felt it, in his bones. It was a perception with him. But there was no science in it; no reasoning. Every detail stood by itself, and had to be learnt either by trial and error or by tradition.

This was the case with all dimensions. I knew how to 'line out' a pair of shafts on a plank, and had in fact lined and helped saw on the saw-pit hundreds of them, years before I understood, thinking it over, why this method came right. So too it was years before I understood why a cart-wheel needed a certain convexity although I had seen wheels fall to pieces for want of it. It was a detail most carefully attended to by the men in my shop; but I think none of them, any more than myself, could have explained why it had to be so.

Some things I never learnt at all, they being all but obsolete even in that primitive shop. To say nothing of square-tongued wheels – a mystery I still think of with some awe – there was the placing of the 'tines' in a wooden harrow that remained an unknown secret to me. The opportunities of investigating it had been too few when cast-iron harrows, ready-made, banished the whole subject from our attention. I just learnt how the harrow was put together to be hauled over the field by one corner; but the trick of mortising the teeth – the 'tines' – into it so that no two cut the same track – this was known to one elderly man but never to me. The same man also failed to teach me how to 'line out' a wooden axle. Indeed, he forgot it himself at last. So it happened that when an ancient dung-cart arrived, needing a wooden axle for its still serviceable wheels, nobody was quite sure how to mark out the axle on the bone-hard bit of beech that was found for it. It was then that my rather useless schooling came in handy for once. With a little geometry I was able to pencil out on the beech the outlines of an axle to serve (in its clumsier dimensions) the better-known purposes of iron. Yet I have no doubt that the elderly wheel-wright's tradition would have been better, if only he could have remembered it.

I Remember, I Remember

BY THOMAS HOOD (1799-1845)

Thomas Hood wrote both serious and humorous
poetry (often the two were intertwined).
During his lifetime, Hood's serious poetry
met less recognition than it deserved, but his
humorous and punning verse attracted much
attention and settled the way in which he
would occupy most of the rest of his life

I remember, I remember,
The house where I was born,
The little window where the sun
Came peeping in at morn;
He never came a wink too soon,
Nor brought too long a day,
But now, I often wish the night
Had borne my breath away!

I remember, I remember,
The roses, red and white,
The vi'lets, and the lily-cups,
Those flowers made of light!
The lilacs where the robin built,
And where my brother set
The laburnum on his birthday —
The tree is living yet!

I remember, I remember,
Where I was used to swing,
And thought the air must rush as fresh
To swallows on the wing;

My spirit flew in feathers then,
That is so heavy now,
And summer pools could hardly cool
The fever on my brow!

I remember, I remember,
The fir trees dark and high;
I used to think their slender tops
Were close against the sky:
It was a childish ignorance,
But now 'tis little joy
To know I'm farther off from heav'n
Than when I was a boy.

'Old House (Ivy Cottage) Shoreham' (1831-2) by Samuel Palmer (1805-81); watercolour plus body colour. (*Ashmolean Museum, Oxford*)

Broken Memories

BY EDWARD THOMAS (1878-1917)

Edward Thomas was encouraged by his friend David Frost to turn to poetry shortly before the First World War. Earlier he had been chiefly engaged in biographical and topographical writing. He was killed on active service in France in 1917

Mr —, the well-known merchant, is building a fine house, half a mile from the — Road. Close upon two acres of woodland have been felled, where, by the way, the largest and juiciest blackberries I know used to be found.

London Local Newspaper

AND in this way many suburbans have seen the paradise of their boyhood effaced. The building rises during some long farewell, and steals away a fraction of the very sky in which once we beheld Orion sink down like a falling sword into the west and its line of battlemented woods. Only here and there a coppice will survive, blockaded by houses a-row. Sometimes a well-beloved pleasaunce is left almost as it was; the trees are the same; the voices are the same; a silence is there still; but there is a caret somewhere – in ourselves or in the place. In childhood we went there as often as our legs could bear us so far; often yet in youth; but less and less with time. Then, perhaps, we travel – anyway we live feverishly and variously; and

only think of the old places when the fire is tranquil and lights are out, and 'each into himself descends', or when we meet one who was once a friend, or when we lay open a forgotten drawer. A very slender chain only binds us to the gods of forest and field – but binds us nevertheless. Then we take the old walk, it may be, in a walking-suit of the best; fearful of mire; carrying a field-glass too; and smoking the pipe that used to seem an insult so intolerable in the great woods. We take the old walk, and it seems shorter than before, a walk not formidable at all, as it was in the years when the end used to find us testy with fatigue and overpowered by tumultuous impressions; when we ourselves thought the sea itself could not be far, and the names of village and hill we visited were unknown.

A railway bisects the common we cross. Everything is haggard and stale; the horizon is gone; and the spirit chafes and suffocates for lack of it. (But the gorse is in flower still.) Then the feet weary on gravel paths downhill. On either side are fields, edged by flaccid suburban grass, with an odour as of tombs – as though nothing fair could blossom in a soil that must be the sepulchre of many divinities. And again the pathway is dogged by houses, interrupting the fields. The former sanity and amenity of air is gone. We can no longer shorten the way to the next houses by a path from the willowy riverside over fields, for the willows are down, the fields heavily burdened with streets. Another length of mean houses, neither urban nor rustic, but both, where I remembered the wretched children's discordant admiration of the abounding gold hair of a passer-by; and soon the bridge over a railway gives a view across plantations of cabbage, etc. But the view is comforting – there is an horizon! There is an horizon barred with poplar trees to the south; the streets are behind, in the north. The horizon is dear to us yet, as the possible home of the unknown and the greatly desired, as the apparent birthplace and tomb of setting and rising suns; from under it the clouds mount, and under it again they return after crossing the sky. A mystery is about it as when we were children playing upon a broad, treeless common, and actually long continued running in pursuit of the horizon.

After three miles in all we leave the turnpike, to follow a new but grassy road out among the fields, under lines of acacia and poplar and horse-chestnut last. Once more the ploughland shows us the twinkling flight of peewits; the well, and the quaking water uplifted in a shining band where it touches the stones; the voices of sparrows while the trees are dripping in the dawn; and overhead the pompous mobilisation of cloud armadas, so imposing in a country where they tilt against ebony boughs ... In a thicket some gypsies have encamped, and two of them – superb youths, with favours of raven hair blowing across the dusky roses of their cheeks – have jumped from their labour to hear the postman reading their letters. Several pipe-sucking bird-catchers are at watch over an expanse of nets. We cross a ploughland half within the sovereignty of the forest shadow. Here is the wood!

The big wood we called it. So well we knew it, and for so many years – wandered here with weeping like Imogen's, and with laughter like Yorick's laughter – that when past years bulk into the likeness of a forest through which the memory takes its pleasure at eventide,

Or in clear dream or solemn vision,

it is really this wood that we see, under a halcyon sky.

It covered two acres in the midst of ploughland; but we thought of it as enormous, because in it we often lost one another; it had such diversity; it made so genuine a solitude. The straight oaks rising branchless for many feet expanded and then united boughs in a firmament of leaves. It seemed far enough from London for feelings of security. But even of that our thoughts have changed; for the houses are fearfully close – a recollection of them lingers in the heart of the wood; and perhaps they will devour it also ... Who shall measure the sorrow of him that hath set his heart upon that which the world hath power to destroy and hath destroyed? Even today the circuit of a cemetery is cutting into the field where we gathered buttercups before the dignity of knickerbockers ... And here was a solitude.

We cannot summon up any thought or reverie which had not in this wood its nativity. 'Tis we have changed! And if we could paint, and wished to make a picture of our youth with its seriousness and its folly, we should paint in this wood, instead of in a hostel-yard, another Don Quixote watching his armour all night after the false accolade.

The dark earth itself was pleasant to handle – earth one might wish to be buried in – and had the healthy and special quality of wild earth: upon it you could rest deliciously. (Compare the artificial soil of a London common with it!) Out of this rose up trees that preserved their wild attitudes. The age-fallen or tempest-uprooted oak-tree lay where it dropped, or hung balanced in the boughs of others. Tenderest bramble spray or feeler of honeysuckle bridged those gaps in the underwood that served as paths. And the winds were husband-men, reapers and sowers thereof. Though, indeed, the trees were ordered with an incongruous juxtaposition of birch and oak and elm, it seemed to us a fragment of the primeval forest left by a possible good fortune at the city verge. But it was more than this. With its lofty roof and the mysterious flashes of light in the foliaged clerestory, with its shapely boles in cluster and colonnade, and the glimpses of bright white sky that came and went among the leaves, the forest had a real likeness to a temple. Shelley's 'Ode to the West Wind' and passages of 'Adonais' were the *ediscenda* of our devotions.

Here we saw the grim jewellery of winter on fallen leaf and bow of grass; gold and purple colouring inseparable from the snow upon boughs overhead; the hills far away sombre and yet white

An illustration by Myles Birket Foster from Thomas Miller's *Birds, Bees and Blossoms*. (*The British Library, London*)

with snow; and on the last of the icy mornings, the sward beaming with melted frost, and the frost only persisting on the ample shadows with which the trees stamp the grass. Here we saw the coming of spring, when the liquid-orbed leaves of toadflax crept out of a barren stone. Full of joy we watched here the 'sweet and twenty' of perfect summer, when the matin shadows were once deleted, and the dew-globes evaporated from the harebell among the fern, or twinkled as they fell silently underfoot. But the favourite of memory is a certain flower-shadowing tree whose branches had been earthbent by the swinging of boyish generations. Foliage and shadow muffled the sight, and seated there in profound emerald moss, the utmost you achieved was to find a name for each of the little thicket flowers. If you raised your head you would have seen in a dainty trefoil, plantain, delicate feathered grasses, starry blossomed heather, illuminations of tormentil, unsearchable moss forests, and there jewelled insects, rosy centaury; nearly all in flower together, and the whole not deep enough to hide a field-mouse.

tumultuous spasm of sunshine – say at mid-March – the blue smoke upcoiling between the boughs of overhanging trees far off and dissipated in the dashing air; the trees singing in their leaflessness like amber and dark agate; above that the woodland seared in black upon the heated horizon blue – but you never raised your head. For hours you could here have peace, among the shadows embroidered with flowers of the colour of gold. All which tantalises – sun and clouds and forever inaccessible horizon – was locked out; only (like a golden bar across a gloomy coat of arms) one sunbeam across the brown wood; thrushes and blackbirds warbled unseen. The soul – this made a cage-bird of it. The eagle's apotheosis in the fires of the sun was envied not. What a subtle diversity of needled herbs and grass there is in the plainest field carpet! all miniature after close cropping of rabbit and sheep; auriferous dandelion, plumed self-heal,

A dim solitude thus circumscribed liked us hugely. We loved not the insolent and importunate splendours of perfect light. Cobwebs and wholesome dust – we needed some of both in the corners of our minds. They mature the wine of the spirit perhaps. We would always have had, as it were, a topmost and nearly inaccessible file of tomes, which we never read, but often planned to read – records peradventure of unvictorious alchemist and astrologer. Thither a sunbeam never penetrated and unmasked. The savour of paraffin and brick-dust should never cling about it. Unfortunate (we thought) is he who has no dusty and never-explored recesses in his mind!

The Dorset Labourer

FROM *LONGMAN'S MAGAZINE*, VOL 2, 1883

Life on the land has changed a good deal since Thomas Hardy's time, and the days when a farmworker went to a hiring-fair are long past. When Hardy wrote 'The Dorset Farm Labourer', which appeared in *Longman's Magazine* in 1886 and from which the following extract is taken, the lot of the farmworker had already improved

TO see the Dorset labourer at his worst and saddest time, he should be viewed when attending a wet hiring-fair at Candlemas, in search of a new master. His natural cheerfulness bravely struggles against the weather and the incertitude; but as the day passes on, and his clothes get wet through, and he is still unhired, there does appear a factitiousness in the smile which, with a self-repressing mannerliness hardly to be found among any other class, he yet has ready when he encounters and talks with friends who have been more fortunate. In youth and manhood this disappointment occurs but seldom; but at threescore and over, it is frequently the lot of those who have no sons and daughters to fall back upon, or whose children are ingrates, or far away.

Here, at the corner of the street, in this aforesaid wet hiring-fair, stands an old shepherd. He is evidently a lonely man. The battle of life has always been a sharp one with him, for, to begin with, he is a man of small frame. He is now so bowed by hard work and years that, approaching from behind, you can scarcely see his head. He has planted the stem of his crook in the gutter, and rests upon the bow, which is polished to silver brightness by the long friction of his hands. He has quite forgotten where he is, and what he has come for, his eyes being bent on the ground. 'There's work in en,' says one farmer to another, as they look dubiously across; 'there's work left in en still; but not so much as I want for my acreage.' 'You'd get en cheap,' says the other. The shepherd does not hear them, and there seem to be passing through his mind pleasant visions of the hiring successes of his prime – when his skill in ovine surgery laid open any farm to him for the asking, and his employer would say uneasily in the early days of February, 'You don't mean to leave us this year?'

But the hale and strong have not to wait thus, and having secured places in the morning, the day passes merrily enough with them.

The hiring-fair of recent years presents

an appearance unlike that of former times. A glance up the high street of the town on a Candlemas-fair day twenty years or thirty years ago revealed a crowd whose general colour was whity-brown flecked with white. Black was almost absent, the few farmers who wore that shade being hardly discernible. Now the crowd is as dark as a London crowd. This change is owing to the range for cloth clothes which possesses the labourers of today. Formerly they came in smock-frocks and gaiters, the shepherds with their crooks, the carters with a zone of whipchord round their hats, thatchers with a straw tucked into the brim, and so on. Now, with the exception of the crook in the hands of an occasional shepherd, there is no mark of speciality in the groups, who might be tailors or under-takers' men, for what they exhibit externally. Out of a group of eight, for example, who talk together in the middle of the road, one only wears corduroy trousers, two patterned tweed suits with black canvas overalls, the remaining four suits being of faded broad-cloth. To a great extent these are their Sunday suits; but the genuine white smock-frock of Russia duck and the whity-brown one of drabbet, are rarely seen now afield, except on the shoulders of old men. Where smocks are worn by the young and middle-aged, they are of blue materials. The mechanic's 'slop' has also been adopted; but a mangy old cloth coat is preferred; so that often a group of these honest fellows on the arable has the aspect of a body of tramps up to some mischief in the field, rather than its natural tillers at their work.

That peculiarity of the English urban poor (which M. Thaine ridicules and unfavourably contrasts with the taste of the Continental working people) – their preference for the cast-off clothes of a

West Country agricultural workers, 1909. (*Radio Times Hulton Picture Library*)

richer class to a special attire of their own – has, in fact, reached the Dorset farm folk. Like the men, the women are, pictorially, less interesting than they used to be. Instead of the wing bonnet like the tilt of a wagon, cotton gown, bright-hued neckerchief, and strong flat boots and shoes, they (the younger ones at least) wear shabby millinery bonnets and hats with beads and feathers, 'material' dresses, and boot-heels almost as foolishly shaped as those of ladies of highest education.

Having 'agreed for a place' as it is called, either at the fair or (occasionally) by private intelligence, or (with growing frequency) by advertisement in the penny local papers, the terms are usually reduced to writing; though formerly a written agreement was unknown, and is now, as a rule, avoided by the farmer if the labourer does not insist upon one. It is signed by both, and a shilling is passed to bind the bargain. The business is then settled, and the man returns to his place of work, to do no more in the matter till Lady Day, Old Style – 6 April.

Of all the days in the year, people who love the rural poor of the south-west should pray for a fine day then. Dwellers near the high-ways of the country are reminded of the anniversary surely enough. They are conscious of a disturbance of their night's rest by noises beginning in the small hours of darkness, and intermittently continuing till daylight – noises as certain to recur on that particular night of the month as the voice of the cuckoo on the third or fourth week of the same. The day of fulfilment has come, and the labourers are on the point of being fetched from the old farm by carters of the new. For it is always by wagon and horses of the farmer who requires his services that the hired man is conveyed to his destination and that this may be accomplished within the day is the reason that the noises begin so soon after midnight. Suppose the distance be an ordinary one of a dozen or fifteen miles. The carter at the prospective place rises 'when Charles's Wain is over the new chimney', harnesses his team of three horses by lantern light, and proceeds to the present home of his coming comrade. It is the passing of these empty wagons in all directions that is heard breaking the stillness of the hours before dawn. The aim is usually to be at the door of the removing household by six o'clock, when the loading of goods at once begins; and at nine or ten the start to the new home is made. From this hour till one or two in the day, when the other family arrives at the old house, the cottage is empty, and it is only in that short interval that the interior can be in anyway cleaned and lime-whitened for the new comers, however dirty it may have become, or whatever sickness may have prevailed among members of the departed family.

Should the migrant himself be a carter there is a slight modification in the arrangements, for carters do not fetch carters, as they fetch shepherds and general hands. In this case the man has to transfer himself. He relinquishes charge of the horses of the old farm in the afternoon of 5 April, and starts on foot the same afternoon for the new place. There he makes the acquaintance of the horses which are to be under his care for the ensuing year, and passes the night sometimes on a bundle of clean straw in the stable, for he is as yet a stranger here, and too indifferent to the comforts of a bed on this particular evening to take much

A farm labourer wearing the traditional smock, c 1857. From *Grundy's English Views*.
(*Radio Times Hulton Picture Library*)

trouble to secure one. From this couch he uncurls himself about two o'clock a.m. (for the distance we have assumed), and, harnessing his new charges, moves off with them to his old home, where, on his arrival, the packing is already advanced by the wife, and loading goes on as before mentioned.

The goods are built up on a wagon to a well-nigh unvarying pattern, which is probably as peculiar to the country labourer as the hexagon to the bee. The dresser, with its finger-marks and domestic evidences thick upon it, stands importantly in front, over the backs of the shaft horses, in its erect and natural position, like some Ark of the Covenant, which must not be handled slightingly or overturned. The hive of bees is slung up to the axle of the wagon, and alongside it the cooking pot or crock, within which are stowed the roots of garden flowers. Barrels are largely used for crockery and budding gooseberry bushes are suspended by the roots; while on the top of the furniture a circular nest is made of the bed and bedding for the matron and children, who sit there through the journey. If there is no infant in arms, the woman holds the head of the clock, which at any exceptional lurch of the wagon stikes one, in thin tones. The other object of solicitude is the looking-glass, usually held in the lap of the eldest girl. It is emphatically spoken of as *the* looking-glass, there being but one in the house, except possibly a small shaving-glass for the husband. But labouring men are not much dependent upon mirrors for a clean chin. I have seen many men shaving in the chimney corner, looking into the fire; or, in summer, in the garden, with their eyes fixed upon a gooseberry-bush, gazing as steadfastly as if there were a perfect reflection of their image – from which it would seem that the concentrated look of shavers in general was originally demanded rather by the mind than by the eye. On the other hand, I knew a man who used to walk about the room all the time he was engaged in the operation, and how he escaped cutting himself was a marvel. Certain luxurious dandies of the furrow, who could not do without a reflected image of themselves when using the razor, obtained it till recently by placing the crown of an old hat outside the window-pane, then confronting it inside the room and falling to – a contrivance which formed a very clear reflection of a face in high light.

The day of removal, if fine, wears an aspect of jollity, and the whole proceedings is a blithe one. A bundle of provisions for the journey is usually hung up at the side of the vehicle, together with a three-pint stone jar of extra strong ale; for it is as impossible to move house without beer as without horses. Roadside inns, too, are patronised, where, during the halt, a mug is seen ascending and descending through the air to and from the feminine portion of the household at the top of the wagon. The drinking at these times is, however, moderate, the beer supplied to travelling labourers being of a preternaturally small brew; as was illustrated by a dialogue which took place on such an occasion quite recently. The liquor was not quite to the taste of the male travellers, and they complained. But the landlady upheld its merits. 'Tis our own brewing, and there is nothing in it but malt and hops,' she said, with rectitude. 'Yes, there is,' said the traveller. 'There's water.' 'Oh! I forgot the water,' the landlady replied. 'I'm d – d if you did, mis'ess,' replied the man;

'for there's hardly anything else in the cup.'

Ten or a dozen of these families, with their goods, may be seen halting simultaneously at an out-of-the-way inn, and it is not possible to walk a mile on any of the high roads this day without meeting several. This annual migration from farm to farm is much in excess of what it was formerly. For example, on a particular farm where, a generation ago, not more than one cottage on an average changed occupants yearly, and where the majority remained all their lifetime, the whole number of tenants were changed at Lady Day just past, and this though nearly all of them had been new arrivals on the previous Lady Day. Dorset labourers now look upon an annual removal as the most natural thing in the world, and it becomes with the younger families a pleasant excitement. Change is also a certain sort of education. Many advantages accrue to the labourers from the varied experience it brings, apart from the discovery of the best market for their abilities. They have become shrewder and sharper men of the world, and have learnt how to hold their own with firmness and judgement. Whenever the habitually-removing man comes into contact with one of the old-fashioned stationary sort, who are still to be found, it is impossible not to perceive that the former is much more wide awake than his fellow-worker, astonishing him with stories of the wide world comprised in a twenty miles radius from their homes.

They are also losing their peculiarities as a class; hence the humorous simplicity which formerly characterised the men and the unsophisticated modesty of the women are rapidly disappearing or lessening, under the constant attrition of lives mildly approximating to those of workers in a manufacturing town. It is the common remark of villagers immediately above the labouring class, who know the latter well as personal acquaintances, that 'there are no nice homely workfolk now as there used to be'. There may be, and is, some exaggeration in this, but it is only natural that, now different districts of them are shaken together once a year and redistributed, like a shuffled pack of cards, they have ceased to be so local in feeling or manner as formerly, and have entered on the condition of inter-social citizens, whose city stretches the whole county over. Their brains are less frequently than they once were 'as dry as the remainder biscuit after a voyage', and they vent less often the result of their own observations than what they have heard to be the current ideas of smart chaps in towns. The women have, in many districts, acquired the rollicking air of factory hands. That seclusion and immutability, which was so bad for their pockets, was an unrivalled fosterer of their personal charm in the eyes of those whose experiences had been less limited.

But the artistic merit of their old condition is scarcely a reason why they should have continued in it when other communities were marching on so vigorously towards uniformity and mental equality. It is only the old story that progress and picturesqueness do not harmonise. They are losing their individuality, but they are widening the range of their ideas and gaining in freedom. It is too much to expect them to remain stagnant and old-fashioned for the pleasure of romantic spectators.

Notes on Illustrations

Sources of most of the pictures used to illustrate *In the Country* are given in the captions. However, it was not possible to include full details for some illustrations, but these are given below:

The introductory drawings at the heads of features were made by Joyce Smith and David Dowland. Other uncaptioned illustrations are by Birket Foster and are from *Birds, Bees and Blossoms* (1858) or *English Country Life* (1859), both by Thomas Miller.

The engraving of the sower on page 10 is by Thomas Bewick; it first appeared in *A Spring Day* by James Fisher, published in 1819.

Flower illustrations on pages 43, 44, 45 and 90 are from the late-nineteenth-century sketch book of M. E. Morris. They appear in this book by courtesy of the Victoria and Albert Museum, London, and were photographed by Brian Hunt of John R. Freeman & Co.

The engravings that appear on pages 75, 78 and 79 were found in *The Illuminated Magazine* that existed from 1843 to 1845.

The small engravings by Birket Foster on pages 97, 101, 102 and 103 appeared in a tiny book entitled *Memento of the Trosacks, Loch Katrine and the Neighbouring Scenery*, by Birket Foster, and published in 1854. The views depicted are those that Dorothy Wordsworth and her brother William would have seen on their tour in Scotland.

The drawing of 'Tom' on page 115 is by Mabel Lucy Attwell and comes from an edition of Charles Kingsley's *The Water Babies*, published by Raphael Tuck & Sons Ltd.

The picture of a hedgehog on page 163 was made by the well-known engraver Thomas Bewick (1753-1828). It appeared in an 1876 edition of Gilbert White's *Natural History of Selborne*.